T0262465

Talk about the Passion

and

Rattlesnakes

Graham Farrow received a Commonwealth Writers' Prize nomination for his first novel *Speak No Evil*, published in 1989. A year later, his first play, *Hair of the Dog*, a piece set in the aftermath of a nuclear holocaust, was premiered by Impact Theatre, Middlesbrough. Eight years and further productions later it was revived at the Birds Nest Theatre, London, to great acclaim. Further plays include *Down amongst the Dead Men* (London, 1993), *The Boys Are Back in Town* (Salisbury, 1994), *Rattlesnakes* (New York, 2001), which is currently in development as an ITV two part television serial, and the award-winning and critically acclaimed *Talk About the Passion*. His new play, *Lake of Fire*, is scheduled to premiere in Michigan in 2005, and his short film script, *Kissing a Fool*, will be filmed in 2005 in New York.

For Dad and David: two of the good guys

Talk about the Passion

and

Rattlesnakes

Graham Farrow

Methuen Drama

Published by Methuen 2004

1 3 5 7 9 10 8 6 4 2

First published in 2004 by
Methuen Publishing Limited
215 Vauxhall Bridge Road
London SW1V 1EJ

Methuen Publishing Limited Reg. No. 3543167

A CIP catalogue record for this book is available from
the British Library

ISBN 0 413 77479 1

Typeset by Country Setting, Kingsdown, Kent

Contents

Talk about the Passion

Talk about the Passion was first performed at the Birds Nest Theatre, London, in May 1998, with the following cast:

Jason Carroway   Damon Unwin
Evelyn Ayles   Marianne Sheehan

Directed by Pippa Dowse

Lights rise inside a working office. **Evelyn Ayles** *stands at her manuscript-littered desk holding a cordless phone. She strides the stage, holding court, her arrogance almost tripping her up.*

Evelyn Now this is the book about them which no one else would dare write whilst they were both still alive. That's what I thought . . . course we could rush it through for an Easter launch . . . okay, I'll hold . . . (*Pauses, flicks through a manuscript, presses number on phone.*) Jenny, before you go, have you sent those figures to the States? It's okay, I'll check my messages before I go. Mr Carroway? He's still here? What part of 'No' doesn't he understand? Look, it doesn't matter, just send him in and I'll deal with him . . . I'll spit him out by six-thirty. I'll lock up, so if you want to go now, that's fine. Yeah. Eight-thirty sharp tomorrow, we've a lot to do before tomorrow lunch. Right – okay . . .

Moments later, **Jason Carroway** *enters carrying a script and a holdall.* **Evelyn** *barely entertains him. She dismissively points him to one of two chairs. He sits, watching her. After a few moments of inactivity he rises, picks up his script and walks towards* **Evelyn**. *Just as he prepares to put the script on her desk, she begins talking again, still looking away from him. He sits.*

Evelyn Yes, I'm still here. We don't know yet, are you scared? (*Begins to stride the stage.*) Why not? (*Laughs.*) They're both dead . . . Do you want me to put out the feelers? I do have one or two cards up my sleeve, but I'm still searching so we'll just have to wait and see. My last one's still a bestseller actually. Well, a car and a driver to and from work would be nice . . . a cottage in the Cotswolds. If you're joking about that I'll go back to Simon and Schuster. Okay then, see you later . . . bye . . . (*She eventually sits and talks to him.*) Well, I must say I really feel that you wasted your time in coming here today, Mr Carroway . . . that's why I sent the script back to you after I read it. (*Flicks through it.*) It er . . . I felt it had a nice light touch, but I . . . I feel that the novel didn't quite live up to the synopsis you gave it. Some of the dialogue worked . . . was pretty taut, but at the end of the day I just feel, Mr Carroway, that you moved into cliché territory . . .

Carroway *remains silent, shifts awkwardly in his seat.*

Evelyn   Perhaps you have to be more ruthless . . . less . . . you know, less emotion and more . . . you know, more story.

Carroway *rises, still silent.*

Evelyn   Does that help at all?

Carroway *nods, walks away, picks up his jacket, puts it on, slowly, meticulously buttons it up. He looks at her, picks up his holdall and exits, his script clutched to him. Pause as* **Evelyn** *picks up another manuscript and reads.*

Moments later **Carroway** *returns, striding purposefully onto stage; altogether a different proposition. He places his holdall beside a chair.*

Carroway   Happiness is a myth . . .

Evelyn (*startled*)   I'm sorry?

Carroway (*pointing to manuscript*)   On the preface . . . something my grandmother used to say to me . . .

Evelyn   Mr Carroway, I'm a very busy woman and I –

Carroway   Clichés?

Evelyn   I'm afraid there is nothing more I can do to help you.

Carroway   Yes there is. Clichés . . . you call my characters clichés. I'm sorry, but those people are real . . . you meet them every time you walk down the street –

Evelyn   I'm simply saying why I –

Carroway   No, no, no. Listen to me for a minute.

Evelyn *shifts uneasily in her seat and checks her watch again.*

Carroway   Can you imagine what sort of person wrote that sort of manuscript? Huh . . . can you? A person who writes about death, misery, grief . . . bloodshed? Do you think maybe that person's unhappy . . . maybe he wants to set the record straight?

Evelyn   Well, I suppose so. Look, I . . . perhaps if you –

Carroway (*moving forward, voice rising slightly*)   Do you think it might be some sort of therapy . . . exorcise some ghosts? (*Getting angry.*) All the emotion poured onto those pages came from here. (*Thumps chest.*) Don't you see, this is no hobby, no twobit pastime . . . this . . . this is my life –

Evelyn   Your life?

Carroway (*becoming upset*)   – on those pages, and you talk about clichés. I was going to keep a diary, but it wasn't enough. I needed . . . needed to have a happy ending.

Evelyn (*tentative*)   So you're Nick? That's you in there?

Carroway   I . . . I had to keep him with me somehow.

Evelyn   Him?

Carroway   No, a diary just wasn't enough. I couldn't rid myself of all . . . all the guilt and sorrow like that. I had to save the day . . . had to turn back the clock and stop the . . .

Evelyn *rises dismissively and turns away, which enrages* **Carroway**.

Carroway   SIT DOWN PLEASE . . . (*Slight pause.*) Just sit down . . . (*He sits, running hands through hair.*) Please . . . sit down . . .

Evelyn   I can see you're upset, but I'm going to have to ask you to leave.

Carroway   Leave?

Evelyn   Well, there's nothing more that I can do to help you.

Carroway   Oh, you're gonna help me all right. You're not going anywhere till we talk.

Evelyn   I really don't have the time for this now.

Carroway   You don't like that manuscript . . . don't want to talk about it because you don't want it to happen to you? Sweep it under the carpet and let some other poor sod deal with it, eh? It frightened you, didn't it, Ms Ayles, eh? *The Wishing Well* frightened you because it's a real story, could happen to anyone . . . not some . . . some cosy Mills and Boon you can read in the garden then toss in the rubbish bin with the weeds and dead plants, no . . . this story is everywhere around us, as soon as we finish our breakfast and step outside that big white front door. You rejected that piece of work because it represents everything that's wrong with society, didn't you?

Evelyn   I've already told you why I rejected it, so if you'll excuse me I have a rather busy schedule.

Carroway   I've told you, I'm not going anywhere till we talk.

Evelyn *goes to pick up phone.* **Carroway** *lunges forward and rips out chord.* **Evelyn** *rises and moves across stage.*

Evelyn   You can't do this to me.

Carroway (*following her*)   Let's talk about clichés.

Evelyn *exits left stage and bangs on door, calling out Jenny's name.* **Carroway** *slips out of his jacket, places it around chair and sits, nonchalantly playing with the key in his hand.* **Evelyn** *returns moments later, flustered and angry. She sits on desk.*

Evelyn   Why are you doing this to me? What do you want?

Carroway   I want you to sit down and listen.

Evelyn   Listen to what? About what?

Carroway   About my son.

Evelyn   Your son? The novel . . . the diary . . . is this about your son? Was he the boy in the manuscript? You *are* Nick, aren't you? And . . . and your boy died, didn't he?

Carroway *applauds facetiously.*

Evelyn   How old?

Carroway *rises and moves towards* **Evelyn**. *He retrieves a wallet from his back pocket and motions for* **Evelyn** *to look at a photo.*

Carroway (*voice wavering with emotion*)   Six-year-old blue-eyed blond ninja-turtle fan with a passion for prawn cocktail crisps. He was my pride and joy, the light of my life, but now he's dead.

Evelyn   How did he die?

Carroway   I lost him and I've lost everything and everyone. You die yourself, you know. My wife . . . (*Pauses as he brings out wallet again and shows her.*) My wife . . . there look . . . she, she blames me, you know . . . if I hadn't let go of his hand. It's the way she looks at me . . . those eyes tear into me . . . they scream at me. (*Slight pause.*) It's funny how you lose your looks when something like that happens . . . how your hair becomes greasy and you get those little pimples popping out all over your face. You wear the same clothes for days on end and you smell so bad that even the dogs won't go near you. You're at the doctor's six, seven times a week and he fills you with so many pills you rattle all the way home. (*Sits.*) You sit down and stare at the telly, but you can't remember what you're watching . . . was it *Home and Away* or *Top of the Pops*? All you see is the video, the one where you suddenly realise he hasn't got hold of your hand and you panic and start to run. You don't know where the hell to go, but you do it all the same. I'd stopped for a sly fag and

Evelyn   So he ran off. Was it a car . . . a van?

Carroway (*calm and composed*)   My son . . . my son was murdered Ms Ayles.

Evelyn (*shocked*)   Murdered?

Carroway (*rising, bitter*)   I turned my back for a second. (*Distant.*) A second . . . that's all . . . a second that'll last the rest of my life. Some pervert was waiting in the bushes for him and –

Evelyn (*turning away from him*)   Please, I don't want to hear this.

Carroway   No, I insist. I want you to hear this because I want you to feel how I felt . . . see what I saw. I want to take you by the hand and sit you on those swings. I want you to take a look into those woods.

Evelyn No . . . no, I can't.

Carroway I want you to smell the fear. (*Pause, moves closer to her.*) Do you know something, I didn't even hear him scream, and by God he must have screamed after what that guy did to him –

Evelyn (*retching*) I'm going to be sick.

Carroway (*following her, directly behind her, towards right stage exit*) They found him two days later . . . stark naked . . . black and blue . . . his Thomas the Tank Engine underpants stuffed in his mouth. (*Points a finger at her blond hair, almost touching the strands.*) The son of a bitch had beaten him so hard there wasn't a single blond strand left on his head. Can you imagine being told that he'd been buggered so hard that his little bowel had been twisted? Can you –

Carroway *breaks off as* **Evelyn** *runs past him towards exit.*

Evelyn I have to leave . . . I have to –

Carroway *grabs her tightly, holds onto her, then throws her roughly onto a chair.*

Carroway Please, please, please sit down. Please, just sit . . . sit down and listen. (*He pushes her against back of chair and sits opposite her, watching her.*) You think my words are offensive . . . savage . . . disgusting, but they're only words. You should've stared at the body . . . should've counted the wounds . . . then you'd know . . . you should've been there . . .

He lunges out again and twists her arms, makes her feel his pain. She cries out in pain, clearly terrified.

I want you to sit with me in court and have the whole world listen to what happened whilst . . . whilst that animal sits there leering at me. (*He frees himself from her and sits upright.*)

Evelyn Why are you doing this to me?

Carroway   Because you're to blame.

Evelyn (*astonished*)   Blame . . . me . . . why? What have I done?

Carroway   Because of you . . . because of all this . . . (*Waves his arms around.*)

Carroway *rises, points to shelves, to manuscripts on her desk and underneath her desk.*

Carroway   It's because of all this . . . all this money . . . this power. My son is dead because of you.

Evelyn   I . . . I just . . . I just don't understand . . . don't understand any of this.

Carroway *rises and paces the office. He checks the books on the shelves, on her desk, rakes through a section of paperbacks in a large box under her desk.*

Carroway   Where is it?

He paces the floor, checking everywhere, pounds the stage like a lion.

Where is it?

Evelyn   What?

Carroway (*screaming*)   WHERE IS IT?

He then systematically trashes the room and the manuscripts. He lifts a box, makes as if he will throw it at her, then throws it against far wall. Moments later, slightly calmer, he paces floor, stops before her and whispers.

Carroway (*almost face to face with her*)   Where is it?

Evelyn (*flustered*)   I don't . . .

He moves towards desk and sits on it, his legs swinging from side to side. He claps his hands, leans forward slightly.

Carroway   Let me make this a little easier for you . . . (*Dramatically clears throat.*) . . . What . . . what is your best-selling title at the moment . . . non fiction?

Evelyn   It's . . . it's er . . . a . . . well, a controversial story . . . the confessions of a mass murderer or . . . or a serial killer, whatever you want to call it. The first-hand account of –

Evelyn *pauses when the realisation sinks in.*

Carroway   Getting warm?

Evelyn   Oh no . . .

Carroway   I'm sorry?

Evelyn (*whispering*)   Oh my God, Miller . . . (*Distant.*) Ryan Miller . . .

Carroway *jumps from desk and walks towards her. He suddenly thrusts out a hand.* **Evelyn** *eyes it suspiciously.*

Evelyn   What . . . I –

Carroway   Pleased to meet you . . . Mick Miller . . . (*He pushes hand forward.*) I said pleased to meet you. Afraid I cheated a bit with the name, but I guess it would've spoilt the surprise otherwise, eh?

He hoves hand fiercely into **Evelyn**'*s ribs. Tearfully she gingerly goes to shake his hand, but he crudely pulls it away at point of contact.*

Carroway   I always wanted to meet the woman who made my son's killer a celebrity. 'S funny, I expected to see someone with horns sticking out of her –

Evelyn (*rising abruptly, slapping out at him, forcing him away from her, tearful*)   SHUT UP SHUT UP SHUT UP. I CAN'T . . . CAN'T STAND THIS. I CAN'T TAKE ANY MORE OF THIS. YOU'VE DRAINED ME . . . I CAN'T HEAR THIS ANY MORE . . . (*Quieter, sitting.*) I can't . . . I just can't.

Carroway *circles her as she speaks. She staggers towards front of stage.* **Carroway** *stands against his chair.*

Carroway   You gave that son of a bitch a total free rein. We had no platform . . . nobody sought our view. You put

him up there, you used his every word and you turned him
into a star, and for that, Evelyn Ayles, you should rot in hell
with him. (*Pauses, sinister.*) Suppose . . . suppose I took you
out right here, right now . . . say I have a handgun here
in my pocket. (*He pauses, slips a hand into his inside pocket
tantalisingly, leaves it there for a few moments. He brings out only an
imaginary gun.*) Would your boss give me a contract? Would
he get Day Lewis to play me in the mini-series? (*He strides the
stage, acting out a bizarre Hollywood mogul's fantasy, chomping on a
cigar, clapping his hands etc.*) Oh yeah, this guy, right, his son's
killed, right, yeah, he writes a novel, gets rejected by the
publishers who made a million for his son's killer. Yeah, but
wait a minute, the best part's when the guy holds the editor
hostage, tortures her, snaps her neck like a fucking chicken
bone, tops her. Oh, I love it, can we get thirty mill to make
it? Maybe we could get parts for Brad and Jennifer. (*Pauses,
reverts to normal tone.*) It's all down to money, isn't it? Did you
for one moment think about us . . . Ryan's family? Is money
so important? Is it? Is it? Answer me?

Carroway *lunges for her, yanks her by the hair and throws her to
the ground. He stands over her.*

Carroway   I said, is money so important? . . .

Evelyn (*shrieking, terrified*)   It wasn't supposed to be like that.
I got a story and they . . . they wanted a new angle. I swear
to God, they took that story, a story from everyone's
viewpoint, and twisted it into . . . into some autobiography.
I swear to God I had no part in any of that. It was a . . .
a look behind his eyes.

Carroway   What about my eyes . . . his mother . . . his
grandparents? Writing that novel – (*Moves over and picks up
manuscript.*) writing *The Wishing Well* was like . . . like an
exorcism . . . like ridding myself of the guilt of not keeping
my eyes open, not holding his hand tightly enough. When
you rejected it, it felt like . . . like you were laughing at me
(*Sarcastically, as if under board-room discussion.*) Hey guys, come
and have a look at this, Mick Miller's having a go at writing.
His writing's as good as his child minding. (*Reverts back to*

normal tone.) I wonder if I'd've put Mick Miller on the manuscript instead of Jason Carroway, I wonder if you'd've taken it.

Evelyn (*gingerly*)   Perhaps if we took another look . . . now that I know the circumstances and –

Carroway (*manic, throws script to the ground*)   FUCK THE MANUSCRIPT. DO YOU HEAR ME, FUCK IT. I EXORCISED MY GHOSTS AND IT'S OVER . . . THE NOVEL MEANS NOTHING. I CAME HERE TO SEE YOU . . . TO SEE WHAT SORT OF PERSON YOU ARE . . . TO SEE THE MONSTER WHO COULD PROFIT FROM THAT HELL AND . . . AND STILL SLEEP AT NIGHT. (*Quieter.*) Just wanted to see what sort of person you are, eh . . .

He lunges at her again, wrestles her to the ground, straddles her, hands tight against her throat. She coughs and splutters, tries to knock him away.

Carroway   What sort of person could do all that, eh . . . eh? What sort of monster? . . .

He sits atop her for some moments, simply staring at her, then he retrieves a tie from his back pocket. He tantalisingly dangles it over her face as she tries to pull away.

Carroway   Nice tie, eh . . . what do you think? What do you think, Ms Ayles? Suit me? No, Ms Ayles, not mine, grown out of it. No, this one spans the generations . . . might even stretch as far back as the Boer War. Yes, Ms Ayles, this old beauty has been passed down from generation to generation . . . always a Miller's had it round his neck . . . greatest gift a Miller could have . . . always passed it onto his first born lad. Trouble is, I don't have anyone to pass it on to now do I? Looks good eh . . . silk. Let me see how it looks on you.

He makes as though to strangle her, then simply frees himself from her and moves to his seat, watching her clutch at her throat.

There is silence for a few moments as he puts the tie back into his bag. He sits back, runs fingers through his hair, then dips his hand back into the holdall. He retrieves a lighter which he flicks on and off suggestively. **Evelyn** *raises herself slightly.*

Carroway   How does it feel? Huh? Not very nice is it . . . pain . . . doesn't feel good does it? *(Pause.)* Do you know, the police held me for a whole day . . . they thought I'd done it . . . some shit about most murders being committed by a family member. Yeah, they thought I'd killed him . . . my own flesh and blood. They scraped the muck from my fingernails and got me to jerk off into a test tube. Nobody gave me a brandy and told me to cry. Nobody made me tea and sandwiches and ran me a hot bath. Even when I came out some fingers were still pointing. I was listening to the radio one day and there was this phone-in and all these people were jamming the switchboard asking what the hell I was doing letting a little kid outta my sight. Some suggested I was pissed, stoned even. Some said I must've been arsing around, ignoring him. One woman called and said people like me shouldn't be able to have kids. People like me? Who are people like me? What the hell did I do to deserve all this? First my son is fucked up the arse by some . . . some animal and it's all my fault. This animal becomes a celebrity and it's me – *(Beats chest.)* – who's the outcast. It's me who can't walk the streets. He's sitting inside his palace eating quayle's eggs and getting more pussy than I've had in a lifetime and I'm the one with the arrow over his head. Christ, you'd think it was me who killed him.

Evelyn *(tentatively)*   Did you have any counselling?

Carroway *laughs manically, rising in tempo; it lasts a good few moments, then snaps off suddenly.*

Carroway   No comment.

Evelyn   What do you mean?

Carroway   Well, I spoke to some woman with glasses and a bun in her hair who ummed and ahhed, prodded and probed. She sat back in her Chesterfield, spread her hands across her desk and said, 'Let's talk.' But how would she know? No, Ms Ayles, as far as counselling me, no chance.

Evelyn   You can talk to me.

Carroway   Because I know you. I've come to know all about you . . . how you operate in your seedy little world. No, Ms Ayles, I want to talk to you and you're going to listen to me. You're gonna hear a bit more.

Evelyn   A bit more?

Carroway (*sits closer to her*)   I'm gonna take you further back . . . yes siree, we're going on a magical mystery ride back in time. We're going to go over a few things, dwell on a few things. How's that grab you, Ms Ayles? Huh? Happy? Sad? Tentative? How ya feeling, Ms Ayles? Yeah, let's hear *my* story. Let's talk about the day I was standing in Smith's just watching the people poring over the book . . . the mile-long queues . . . the autographed copies . . . There was this . . . this woman absolutely glued to it . . . she . . . she couldn't take her jam-jar specs away from it. At one point she actually laughed. Laughed, I tell you. Then two lads came in and picked up a copy each. They were reading bits out aloud to each other. One would read a bit, then the other would say, 'Hang on, this bit's worse.' I just stood there and listened to them . . . watched them revelling in it. They were like vultures . . . enjoying it, being entertained by it. I felt like going over and smacking their heads in, but I thought about the headlines in the *Sun* the next day . . . 'Madman father of murdered child causes mayhem in bookshop.' What's the point? I stayed in there so long that the security guard came over and asked me to leave . . . thought I was there to lift a few encyclopaedias. I told him I had a right to be there . . . a right to know which monsters were buying the book, and you know what he said to me? Huh? Do you? Do you?

Evelyn   No.

Carroway   He said he'd a right to go home. Yeah, that's what that fat prick said to me. Said he'd a right to go home. Can you fucking believe that? So I said to him as he frogmarched me outta the shop, I said, hey fucker, I'm

gonna bomb this shop and all the other shops in this
country who are stocking this filth, and you're gonna get
the first blast. So I went home, got pissed and tried to make
a Molotov cocktail . . . ended up setting fire to the garage.
Then I went upstairs, threw up and went to bed. (*Pause.*)
How . . . how can anybody read about somebody else's
suffering and actually enjoy it? That child of mine died
alone and frightened, not knowing what was happening to
him, not being able to understand. Kids who have to die
should be with their parents . . . holding them, reassuring
them . . . cuddling them. I'll never be able to forget that
he died knowing I wasn't there, that I let him down. His
photo stares down at me from the mantelpiece every day
and he says to me – (*Crying.*) 'Where were you, you bastard?
Where . . . were you . . .'

Carroway *cries audibly, painfully, shielding his face.* **Evelyn** *rises
to touch him and he lashes out at her. He sits on farthest chair with
his head in his hands, crying, for some moments. There is an incredible
feeling of tension in the air. Eventually* **Carroway** *rises and moves
towards left stage, front, staring. He turns to* **Evelyn** *and regards her.*

Carroway   Do you dream? You have good dreams, Ms
Ayles? Huh?

Evelyn   Yes . . . yes, I dream.

Carroway   I used to have this dream . . . still do in fact,
that it was all a terrible mistake and I'd come down the
stairs and he'd be at the breakfast bar washing his face with
the milk from his Cheerios. (*Laughs in remembrance.*) He'd start
nagging me about when I'd go and buy his puppy and I'd
sit there and ruffle his hair and tell him he'd better go ask
his mam, her being the boss, you know, then . . . then he'd
change right there in the chair . . . he's suddenly older,
harrassing me to go and kick the ball around in the garden.
He'd get the ball, dribble around me and feign a heart
attack before sticking the ball in the goal. Then he's . . . he's
older still . . . he wants money for a film and a burger . . .
he's taking some good-looker out after the football match . . .
always watches Middlesbrough . . . home and away. Then

he's older still . . . he's playing at the Riverside and he swaps
passes with Juninho before scoring on his debut. I'm in the
crowd with my Boro shirt with 'Miller, Number Seven' on
the back, and I'm telling the guy next to him the new lad's
my Ryan and he's gonna play for England. (*Sings.*) He's
gonna play for England . . . (*Slight pause.*) Then I wake up
and the rain's lashing against the window and I have to get
on with my life.

Evelyn (*tentatively*)   What about your friends?

Carroway   They're funny, you know. There's this distance.
They don't know how to approach you. They see you in the
supermarket and they tap their watches, telling you they're
half an hour late and they'd love to talk but, you know . . .
it's . . . it's like I'm some sort of Jonah. (*Imitates a worried
parent.*) Oh, don't hang around with him, your kids might
get killed as well. Small town . . . everyone knows your
business . . . you can't hide, and people . . . people, when
they see you, they just don't know what to say. Couple of
months later I was standing in the supermarket one day and
I found myself standing in front of the cereal section. I was
just breaking my heart staring at the boxes of Cheerios.
Then I started to put things into my basket . . . didn't
realise . . . stupid things like tins of chick-peas and boxes
and boxes of Bisto. I was like a madman, knocking people
out of the way to get to the shelves. I started putting things
into my pockets, then in my mouth. At one point I was
munching spaghetti sticks and drinking cooking oil. I just
didn't know what I was doing. If someone had come up to
me and told me I was the Queen of Sheba I'd've believed
them. Anyway, this guy comes over and marches me into
this office. They were ready to throw the book at me when
someone says – (*Whispers conspiracy-like.*) ''Ang on a minute,
that's Mick Miller, the guy who's son's been killed,' and they
all smile . . . that sweet, squirmy smile, make me a cup of
tea and give me a complimentary hamper. 'You know, the
guy's nuts, just humour him.' (*Mimes a lunatic. Slight pause,
beings to cry.*) Then . . . then they sent for me dad to come
and fetch me . . . the first thing I thought about when Ryan

was missing wasn't, 'Oh my God my boy's missing,' it was what would my dad think of me. It happened very close to where they live. Dad crossed that park every morning for his paper. Ryan was at that age when he adores his nana and granddad . . . their house being a sweet shop and playground all rolled into one. Dad used to walk him through that park, kick the ball with him and gather conkers. They'd crouch down and watch the squirrels and Ryan would howl with delight whenever he spotted one. I wonder if he saw one before he . . . before he . . . (*Pause.*) I . . . I should've been there for him . . . I should've been there . . . (*Cries again. He walks towards his chair, lashes out at it, then sits down, hands covering his face.*) I should've been there . . .

Evelyn   People don't understand. (*She rises slowly on her knees.*) It's so hard to feel your pain sometimes. Sometimes it's easier to –

Carroway (*looking at her, menacing*)   What?

Evelyn   It's hard for people to –

Carroway   Don't do me any favours. Don't pretend you know what's going on.

Evelyn   Why wouldn't I?

Carroway   You talk as if . . . as if . . . you sit there and talk to me as if –

Evelyn   As if I've been there?

Carroway (*takes the lighter from his pocket and begins to flick it*) Yeah.

Evelyn   I have to have been there . . . I have to have seen hell, then I'd know. Is that it? Is that the point?

Carroway   Bingo.

Evelyn   You think you know me?

Carroway   What?

Evelyn (*flustered*)   Well, you sit there . . . you attack me, abuse me . . . you tell me what I think and how I feel. It's good that you know everything about me because you know how I suffer.

Carroway (*cynical*)   Suffer, you . . . do me a favour. Edit the book . . . exploit people's feelings . . . don't think about suffering, and don't ever pretend you've been there.

Evelyn (*rising, angrily*)   Who do you think you are? You don't know what my life's like . . . what it's been like. You don't know anything at all about me. You . . . you rant and rave about people and hate and pain . . . and . . . but you can't see past your own nose. You are not the only person who has suffered.

Carroway   Mebbe I want other people to suffer like I did. Mebbe I want Roth's family to be pointed at and harrassed . . . mebbe I want reporters camped on their doorsteps and rummaging through their rubbish bins. Mebbe I want telescopic lenses poked towards their toilets, not mine . . . okay? Asking too much, am I?

Evelyn   But they do suffer. You're so full of anger and pain that you can't see other people . . . can't . . . won't listen to them. There's something deep within all of us . . . some secret buried deep down . . . a place where none of us like to return.

Carroway (*angrily*)   And you've been there, have you? (*He pulls his holdall round and unzips it.*) Been there, have you . . . down . . . down there? (*He emerges with a can of petrol, flicks off top.*) Down where we don't like to go but – (*Shouting.*) – WHERE OUR NEIGHBOURS AND OUR ENEMIES LIKE TO GO AND BRING A PIECE OF IT BACK FOR THE TABLOIDS. YOU'VE BEEN THERE, HAVE YOU, MS AYLES?

He lunges for her, forces her to floor, pins her down, **Evelyn** *trying desperately to fend him off.*

Carroway   You've been there eh . . . (*Pours petrol all over her.*) . . . right down there amongst the shit and slime . . . been there, have you?

He pours the petrol over himself, then tosses can. He massages the petrol into her face and hair and brings out the lighter, teasing her with it. As she tries to speak he shakes his head at her and continues to rub the petrol in.

Carroway   Ms Evelyn Ayles . . . been there, have you . . . right down there . . . been there, eh?

All the while she is screaming, kicking out, trying to fend him off.

Evelyn (*still trying to break free, struggling as his hands probe her mouth*)   Look around you . . . what do you see? Where are my photos? You might have come up twenty floors and passed my two secretaries and a PA, but what do I have? What do you see? You see a young woman who's climbed the corporate ladder, but what do you really see? Look around you? Where are my photos? Where is my husband?

Carroway   You got me . . . where?

Evelyn   Where's the joy in my eyes?

Carroway   And the Oscar goes to . . .

Evelyn   What do you see? Fake smile? Can't you see the loneliness? Can't you see how alone I am?

Carroway   You're alone, eh? Who isn't?

Evelyn   I'm alone because I had a child . . .

Carroway   Liar . . . liar . . . pants on fire . . . (*Puts lighter inside her mouth.*)

Evelyn   I had a child growing inside me, but it wasn't planned and I didn't want that child stopping me making lots of money so I decided to terminate it . . .

Carroway *recoils in horror, drags himself away from* **Evelyn** *and moves towards the desk.* **Evelyn** *rises slightly, on her knees.*

Evelyn   . . . There were complications . . . I was haemor-raging badly and they had to operate. I killed my son because I was greedy and I . . . I got the payback. For that greed I could never bear another child. I killed my son and lost my husband soon after and I have to live with that decision every day of my life and it will haunt me till the day I die. So, Mr Carroway, you take a good look into my eyes and tell me I haven't suffered.

Evelyn *staggers upwards, tearful, disorientated.* **Carroway** *is left-stage, panting, holding onto chair, facing floor. His breathing is heavy, uneven. There is a pause as the two reflect on what has passed between them.*

Evelyn (*warily*)   What if . . . what if you stood there in the park and saw him . . . saw Roth just before he grabbed Ryan, and you could kill him there and then?

Carroway   Shut the fuck up.

Evelyn   If . . . if he was there and you knew what he would do . . . you'd read the stories . . . knew he was looking for another victim. What would you –

Carroway (*desperate*)   Shut up . . . just shut up. What the fuck are you talking about, you crazy bitch?

Evelyn   I . . . I know if I could . . . if I could change the past, I would. If I could have that child again –

Carroway (*pacing floor*)   I don't know. You can't bring abortion into it . . . something you did as a silly love-struck teenager. You did that . . . it was your choice. I had no choice.

Evelyn   But I'm saying I would change it. We're still talking about the death of a loved one . . . if I could go back I would . . . you know you would if you could.

Carroway (*angrily*)   What are you talking about? How can you sit there and listen to me then start telling me what I would and wouldn't do? You're talking about an unborn child . . . a . . . a nothing. I'm talking about a loved and loving boy . . . a human being with his own personality . . . his own qualities . . . . his ability to give happiness and love. I'm talking about someone who had everything to live for.

Evelyn   And there's a difference?

Carroway   COURSE THERE'S A FUCKING
DIFFERENCE.

Evelyn   Not to millions of others there isn't a difference.

Carroway   I don't give a shit. You cannot sit there and
advise me to do anything. You are the woman who has
profited from my son's death.

Evelyn (*angrily*)   YOU . . . YOU THINK YOU'VE GOT
SOME SORT OF MONOPOLY ON GRIEF . . . YOU
DON'T KNOW ANYTHING. YOU KNOW I'M RIGHT.
YOU WOULD GO OUT THERE AND KILL ROTH . . .
YOU KNOW THAT AND I KNOW THAT. (*Quietens.*) You
know that.

Carroway   You know nothing . . . you hear me. Nothing.

Evelyn (*moving towards desk, stands behind it*)   I know you
would. Anyone with as much pain . . . as much hatred as
you . . . they would. I know you would because –

Carroway   BECAUSE WHAT?

Evelyn   Because.

Carroway   BECAUSE WHAT . . . COME ON . . .
LEMME HAVE IT . . . BECAUSE WHAT YOU . . .
YOU FUCKING –

Evelyn   BECAUSE YOU'LL GET RESPECT. YOU'LL
GET THAT LOVE BACK. THEY'LL ALL SEE. THEY'LL
ALL KNOW WHAT IT DID TO YOU . . . THEY'RE
WAITING . . . ALL OF THEM WAITING FOR THE
PAYBACK.

Carroway (*slightly offguard, allowing it to sink in, slight pause*)
What, I should go out now and kill him? Is that it? Shall I
stop at him or go right through the whole prison population?

Evelyn (*resigned*)   If he wasn't here . . . if his face wasn't on
the front of a book, then it would be over, wouldn't it? He
wouldn't be there to pick up his royalty cheque or eat his
duck *à l'orange* or whatever. He wouldn't be able to hurt you
any more.

Carroway   Kill him, then serve twenty years for murder myself?

Evelyn   And what jury would convict you, huh?

Carroway   No chance.

Evelyn   I'm telling you, you wouldn't go to jail for an act of revenge. You'll have every person in the country behind you. When you get home they'll keep the pub open all night and they'll crowd round you, patting you, shaking your hand and telling you you've done the right thing. People in this country have had enough of all this crime. Don't you think it might make some other nut sit down and think twice before he goes out to commit a crime if he thought he might have to pay for that crime . . . I mean *really* pay.

Carroway   Maybe in Hollywood.

Evelyn   No, if he committed a crime . . . a heinous crime and thought he might die as a result, don't you think it might affect his decision?

Carroway (*cynical*)   All so simple, huh? And life is as simple as all that, isn't it? What planet have you been living on recently?

Evelyn   You've seen those men in those documentaries . . . they're the ones who've lost sons and daughters to mass murderers. How many of them last into their sixties? It's not only sorrow, it's guilt . . . it's failure . . . the failure not only to protect, but to bring justice.

Carroway   Justice . . . you talk about justice? What justice have I got?

Evelyn   Exactly. What justice does anyone get nowadays?

Carroway   But you can't get away with it. If I . . . if I went out there and killed him, I couldn't get away with it. It's impossible.

Evelyn   What about the others . . . the other kids he killed?

Carroway   The others?

Evelyn (*more confident, begins to move closer to him*)   Think about their families . . . it's not just for you and your family . . . it's for them . . . you're helping them . . . that's the justice. The justice is ridding him from the equation. I mean, what about Danny Williams's father?

Carroway   Danny Williams's father?

Evelyn   He didn't see any justice. He slid downhill really fast . . . only weeks after burying his son in a closed casket. The chest pains hit him straight away and claimed him six months ago. Where's his justice, Mr Miller? And what about Mrs Williams? She's lost two members of her family. Who's going to help her . . . who's there to pick up the pieces for her?

Carroway *says nothing, allowing it all to sink in.*

Evelyn   Justice . . . justice for everyone . . . for all the families. That's all they want . . . all they ask for . . .

Carroway (*distant*)   For them. Maybe I could do it for them.

Evelyn (*nearing him*)   Roth killed your son because it didn't matter to him. He literally thought . . . what the hell. He knew he'd be caught and jailed regardless. A more . . . more callous act, a heavier sentence, more security . . . away from all the angry prisoners with their fists and broken bottles. He knew the law all right, better than any of us, and the saddest piece of this whole conundrum if he hadn't been let out the first time, and if life meant a life of breaking rocks and living on bread and water, or if you were hanged . . . well . . .

Carroway (*through tears*)   Then Ryan would still be alive. He's got nothing to lose and I'm sitting at home seeing ghosts everywhere I turn. (*Pauses.*) Is this . . . is all this in the book? All this detail? Did he actually say all that, about killing meaning nothing to him . . . that it was some sort of decoy for a cosier standard of living?

Evelyn   That . . . that man didn't hold back one iota. He's having his own poke at the public who can't get enough of all this sickness and depravity. He's laying it on with a spatula. If he ever slips up he's got the best lawyers in town ready to stand him up on his feet and slap in a couple of lawsuits for him. Do you know he's actually thinking of launching an appeal . . . on a technicality?

Carroway What? What the –

Evelyn Heard it only last week. And I tell you something, Mr Miller, some guys in this office are taking bets on the outcome. They reckon he's five-to-one to walk off into the sunset . . . towards more playgrounds . . . more parks . . .

Carroway (*incredulous*) He's getting out?

Evelyn It's not certain . . . but . . .

Carroway People are backing him to get out . . . lawyers are helping him? I'm . . . my life is hanging by threads . . . my wife's left me, my fucking father can't look me in the eye, Danny Williams's father's dead and they're talking about fucking appeals? That animal has nothing to lose . . . I don't . . . I just don't –

Carroway *rocks back and forth, clenching his teeth and shaking his head.*

Carroway Fucking appeals . . . I don't . . . just don't –

Evelyn (*goading him*) All those marriage break-ups . . . broken hearts . . . broken communities. Think of the whole area scared out of their wits for the fifteen months he was on the rampage. Can you . . . can you imagine going through that again . . . imagine some other community, some other parents? Your dad?

Carroway Shut up, I can't –

Evelyn Your dad? What would he think of you now? What would he want of you . . . expect of you?

Carroway He'd want me to kill Roth. I'd finally be doing the right thing.

Evelyn Payback

Carroway   When Dad'd go into the Three Swans after Ryan's death, he'd get the look . . . the same one I've had every day of my life. And by Christ, he hated that look. My dad was made to feel ashamed by all his cronies. He'd failed because I'd failed, and in their eyes he was as much to blame as I was. He wasn't welcome in that circle any more.

Evelyn   And failure is the worst thing a proud man can endure?

Carroway   Those boys don't cry and rant and rave . . . they don't sit in front of counsellors and doctors and analysts. They don't fuck around, they act. And . . . and –

Evelyn   And?

Carroway   And they're waiting for me to act. Stop acting like a pussy and carve that fucker up good and proper.

Evelyn   And you're ready.

Slight pause as the words sink in.

Carroway   How do I get him?

Evelyn   You're sure?

Carroway   It's about time.

Evelyn *approaches him, but he pulls back and shoos her away, intimating that he doesn't want to be close to her.*

Evelyn   You won't be able to get inside . . . nigh on impossible . . . certainly won't be able to get a gun in, even if I got you a pass saying you were the new guy on the story. No, it will . . . it will have to be on the outside.

Carroway   How exactly?

Evelyn   Can you get a gun . . . a powerful long-ranger, just in case?

Carroway   I should think so . . . I know somebody who knows somebody and that somebody should be able to teach me how to hit the target.

Evelyn I know . . . every Tuesday he's been having treatment on an abcessed tooth. It was a routine job at first, but he ignored it and it got too bad too fast. They can't do it inside, so he has to be farmed out to a specialist centre . . . guess who's footing the bill? They didn't believe him at first . . . thought he was looking for a way to get out and pull an escape on them. Anyway, he finally persuaded them, they put more security on him than the Royal Family, put him in an armoured van at eleven-thirty on the button and return on the hour . . . not a minute later. You'll have to park around the corner, watch for the return, then move in. You'll get one chance as the van pulls up just outside the gates to drop him off. They don't go inside for some reason . . . just open the smaller steel door and lead him back inside. Two officers will flank him to escort him in. Get in close . . . as close as you can . . . two shots. Drop the gun and let them grab you . . . no histrionics . . .

Carroway Smooth as silk, huh?

Evelyn I don't see why it shouldn't be if you follow my plan to the letter.

Carroway What if someone notices a car parked in the vicinity and a nervous guy loitering around with a large bulge in his pocket?

Evelyn Park as far from the main building as you can . . . leave it in the car park near the hypermarket and walk. Put the gun in the holdall. Maybe you should carry a couple of bags of groceries . . . look like an ordinary shopper. Just discard the bags when you're near him.

Carroway Will anyone recognise me . . . anyone . . . any officers leaving the building or anything?

Evelyn Shouldn't think so. Wear a cap, part your hair down the middle or something . . . grow a beard.

Carroway And two shots?

Evelyn As quick as you can. No fumbling. If you miss this chance, you'll never get another. Don't speak to him, it might throw you. Just get in close and do it. Remember, he's not stupid.

Carroway   And the jailers?

Evelyn   They won't be armed and they'll probably be cuffed to him, at least one of them, anyway. They can't hinder you because of that immobility and he certainly can't hit back. It's all about timing and speed. And remember the element of surprise. They won't be expecting anything . . . it'll be the same Tuesday as the past half-dozen . . . use that surprise to your advantage.

Carroway   And when it's over . . .

Evelyn   Don't scream and don't use any bad language. Don't harrass the jailers in any way and make sure you don't hurt them in the slightest. If you do it all cleanly, then the jury will be more sympathetic. Two shots to the head, drop the gun and stand still. Nobody will hurt you, neither the jailers outside or anybody inside. And don't think for one minute they actually care what happens to this guy . . . there'll be no love lost . . . they know what he did and they know the world will be a safer place once he's gone. In fact, they'll probably have a couple of beers on you down at their local club later that night.

Carroway   Right . . . fine.

Evelyn   Okay, got everything.

Carroway *nods and walks towards her. She moves aside as he picks up the petrol can, screws the top back on and takes it back to his seat. His eyes still fixed on* **Evelyn***, he places the can back into his holdall, zips it up and slips his jacket back on, buttoning it meticulously. He raises the holdall and stands before her. He moves closer, she backs away again.*

Evelyn   Two shots, in close . . . eleven-thirty, back on the hour. When you walk, make sure you don't arouse the suspicions of the van driver . . . keep out of his range. Stick to what I've said and there'll be no problems.

Carroway   Right then . . .

He turns away, pauses, walks towards her again. He nods.

Carroway (*tentatively*)   I'll . . . I'll be in touch.

Evelyn   You do that.

Carroway *exits left stage.* **Evelyn** *goes towards desk, plugs in phone, contemplates calling someone, then places receiver in its cradle. She sits down and places her head in her hands.*

Lights fade.

Lights rise.

Some months later. **Evelyn** *stands at her desk, phone in her hand. She takes a sip of champagne and rummages through all the mail dumped on her desk.*

Evelyn (*excitedly*)   Lloyd, hi, yes . . . Evelyn. Did you see the paper? Let me read it to you . . . the news from the courthouse is that Mr Michael Miller, vigilante killer of mass murderer Mr Steven Roth, was today sentenced to seven years in prison for the cold-blooded slaughter of his son's killer. Although Judge Robert Munroe conceded that Miller was under considerable emotional stress resulting from his son's death, he could in no way condone Miller's actions. Whilst citing that Miller was in no way a danger to the public, the judge commented on the sheer brutality of the slaying, referring to the five shots, one being from close range to the temple, and stressed that he could not let the offence go unpunished, and that vigilantes should not be allowed to play God. Miller himself refuses to talk to reporters, but his campaigners have stated that they will not rest until he is released. More news in later editions, blah de blah de blah . . . yes I know. Amazing huh? I couldn't have asked for a better publicity campaign for the book. What? A title? Well I was thinking . . . *Roth versus Miller: the Whole Story* . . . you do, great. You can have the first signed copy.

(*Laughs.*) Perhaps we'll go for the Pulitzer for this one. What do you mean how did I get the story . . . a great writer never reveals her sources . . . (*Laughs.*) Gotta go, Lloyd . . . people to meet, interviews to do, money to earn. You too, Lloyd. Come down and have a glass of shampoo with me. Okay . . . bye . . . (*Replaces receiver, picks up newspaper again and kisses front page.*) Thank you Mr Miller or Carroway or whatever the hell you call yourself. See you in about five years, matey . . .

She laughs, drinks champagne again. After a few moments she moves to the pile of mail. She opens one or two smaller letters, tuts and tosses them both into the bin, then comes to a large package. She checks it quizzically and unravels it, searches for a letter, finds none. She brings out a Fisher-Price children's tape-recorder. She regards it quizzically again, searches the box for clues, then presses play. We hear nothing, then suddenly, **Carroway**'s *voice appears.*

Carroway Testing . . . testing . . . one, two . . . Hello, Ms Ayles, thought you may find this interesting . . .

There is a slight pause, then we hear **Evelyn**'s *voice on the tape. It is quickly obvious that* **Carroway** *taped the whole previous encounter.*

Evelyn . . . Can you get a gun . . . a powerful long-ranger, just in case? Get in close . . . as close as you can . . . two shots . . . then drop the gun . . . Stick to what I've said and there'll be no problems. Remember, the world will be a safer place without him . . .

The tape tails off with **Evelyn**'s *voice still plotting. She staggers back into her chair and collapses into it, head in hands.*

Lights fade slowly.

End.

Rattlesnakes

Rattlesnakes was first performed by Feed the Herd Theatre Company at the Flatiron Playhouse, New York, in June, 2001, with the following cast:

Robert McQueen Kevin Kaine
Richie Hanson Jamie Benge
Jamie Jarrett Jermaine Chambers
Jed Ellis Jose Armando
Shelly Hanson Arin Quinn

Directed by Brian Snapp

Act One

A pitch-black hotel room; cheap but not seedy. There is a soft rapping at door. No answer. Louder knocking. Lights rise only on doorframe as door opens and a man, **McQueen** *enters, first poking his head round door. He stands still, light illuminating only him.*

Other lights rise slowly, showing two single beds at left side complete with side tables and fridge. A dressing table is situated further up left stage. On the right-hand side is a set of wardrobes.

Suddenly the three wardrobe doors burst open and three hooded men appear holding assorted weapons and holdalls. **McQueen** *shrieks, clearly startled and attempts to leave. Two men leap forward and grab hold of him as he struggles. A man,* **Hanson***, passes them, takes the 'Do Not Disturb' sign from inside, opens door, puts it on outside. He slams door, locks it. All this happens without a single word.*

McQueen *continues to struggle as two men drag him towards a single chair beside the dressing table. The first man,* **Jarrett***, emerges with masking tape, tapes* **McQueen***'s mouth as he protests.* **Ellis***, the second man, watches silently.*

Hanson *saunters towards* **McQueen***, stands before him, watching him. The other two men sit on separate beds.* **Hanson** *walks towards bedside table, lifts receiver from phone. He then moves back towards* **McQueen***, who continues his muffled protest, backing away and lashing out with his feet.* **Hanson** *gestures towards* **Ellis***, who opens his holdall and brings out rope. He ties rope around* **McQueen***'s hands and feet. During this,* **Hanson** *searches through* **McQueen***'s pockets. He emerges with a mobile phone which he smashes to ground and handles an address book which he rifles through.*

There is silence for a few moments. **Ellis** *and* **Jarrett** *sit on beds.* **Hanson** *stands immediately before his prey still reading address book.*

Hanson   Waiting for someone, huh?

He takes a bowie knife from a scabard on his belt, runs a finger along blade. **McQueen** *pulls away, protesting, terrified.* **Hanson** *continues to thumb through address book.*

Hanson   My wife tonight. Jed's . . . (*Refers to book.*) . . . Thursday and Jamie's . . . Sunday. My, my, you are one busy young man, aren't you?

He tosses book on bed where the other two thumb it in turns.

Now, before I cut your throat, I want a coupla answers. Now, seeing as though you're somewhat . . . er . . . detained, you'll nod or shake your head. Okay? Okay?

McQueen *nods.*

Hanson   Now, first question . . . have you been fucking my wife?

McQueen *doesn't shake or nod.* **Hanson** *regards* **Ellis** *and* **Jarrett**, *shrugs, then lunges at* **McQueen**, *slashing his left cheek.* **McQueen** *gives out a muffled scream and falls forward on chair.* **Jarrett** *moves forward and straightens him.* **McQueen** *coughs, splutters, in tears.*

Hanson   I'll ask you again. Have you been fucking my wife?

McQueen *furiously shakes head.*

Hanson   Then why did she book this fucking room and why are you here? Are you the cleaner? Too much like a pretty boy to be a cleaner.

Ellis   Just fucking do him. I can't bear to look at him.

Hanson (*gesturing to* **Jarrett**)   And you?

Jarrett   Kill him. Let him be with Janice . . . he liked her that much, they should be together.

Hanson (*turning to* **McQueen**)   Hear that? Whaddya reckon? D'ya believe this guy? This guy's just said he killed his wife 'cause of you. Is he telling the truth? Whaddya say? (*Laughs.*) Let's be honest, if he killed the mother of his baby, he's not gonna give a flying fuck to see you drown in your own blood. Dilemma, isn't it?

Jarrett   Not to me it isn't.

Ellis   Can you take his gag off? I want some answers . . .
I want some details.

Hanson   If he squeals –

Jarrett   He won't . . . believe me. Obviously his brains are
in his bollocks, but he doesn't look totally stupid.

Hanson (*mulling it over, then to* **McQueen**)   You gonna be a
good boy?

McQueen *nods frantically.* **Hanson** *regards his comrades, then
takes tape off.* **McQueen** *coughs, splutters, regains composure. Silence
for a few moments.*

Ellis (*tossing address book at* **McQueen**)   What's the score,
then?

McQueen (*regarding them warily*)   What can I say?

Hanson   Look, don't fuck around with us. This doesn't
look good for you, does it, so if you've any sense you'll tell
us what the hell's going on.

Jarrett   My fucking patience is about to snap. (*He rises.*)

McQueen   Okay, okay. I . . . I know your wives . . . all
three of them.

Jarrett (*taking pliers from holdall, turns to* **Hanson**)   I told you
what he'd be like didn't I? I'm not having this smug little
prick playing games with me.

He roughly takes hold of **McQueen***'s left hand, spreads it on arm of
chair whilst* **McQueen** *protests.*

McQueen (*terrified*)   Right . . . right. I know your wives
because . . . because . . . I . . . Shit, I . . . I entertain them.

Ellis   You entertain them?

Hanson   You fuck them?

McQueen   No, I entertain them . . . really, I –

Jarrett (*relaxing his hand*)   You entertain my wife? What sort
of fucking answer's that? Who'd ya think you are, Fred Astaire?

Hanson   And this is why my wife used my hard-earned cash to book this shitty middle-a-nowhere hotel, with its fucking flashing red light and cum stained sheets? You're gonna entertain her right here huh? Gonna pull a rabbit out of a hat? 'S that it?

McQueen   It's not like that.

Ellis   Do you always bring them here?

McQueen   No.

Jarrett   What class you've got, eh? How much did that gel in your hair cost . . . (*Circles him, flicking out at* **McQueen**.) What about the suit . . . the tie? Did we pay for that as well?

Ellis   He's a ponce.

Jarrett (*standing over* **McQueen**)   How much do you charge?

McQueen *tuts and turns away.* **Jarrett** *smacks him round the head with pliers. He screams out in pain and rocks back.*

Jarrett   I wouldn't worry about the noise this cunt's gonna make . . . it's probably nothing compared to what the general punter makes in this classy joint. Now answer the question? How much?

McQueen (*coughing, gurgling*)   Depends.

Hanson   By the hour, eh, or is it satisfaction guaranteed or your money back?

McQueen   Depends what they want.

Ellis   What a fucking insult to every man who breaks his balls working twelve hours a day. What an insult to every man who puts himself through hell to feed, clothe and . . . and fucking die for his wife. Fucking ponce in a cheap suit.

McQueen   That's me . . . a real bad man.

Jarrett   Oh, are you being sarcastic? Oh, I think he's trying to make a point, gentlemen. I think he's trying to turn it round and say we're the bad guys.

McQueen   Well, I'm the one in the chair surrounded by men in masks.

They all pause momentarily as if in some internal discussion. Suddenly **Hanson** *removes his mask. After a few moments,* **Ellis** *does the same.*

Jarrett (*still hooded, facing* **McQueen**)   Well, it's not as if you're gonna be able to grass us up, is it? (*He also takes his off.*)

Ellis   I wanna know how long you've been seeing my wife and how it came about. I wanna know how much of my money's lined your pockets.

McQueen   Well, she phoned me up in –

Ellis (*incredulous*)   She what?

McQueen   What, do you think we met in a bar? Do I look like a light-ale man?

Ellis *takes a run at him and kicks him square in the groin.* **McQueen** *shrieks in pain.*

Hanson   What's this phone-call shit? Are you telling us all our wives . . . they all called you and you arranged something? Is that it?

McQueen (*coughing and spluttering*)   I'm a businessman.

Jarrett   A fucking gigolo . . .

McQueen *nods and smirks sarcastically.* **Ellis** *stands there visibly fuming. He roars out his anger and frustration, then lashes out again.* **Hanson** *pulls him away while he kicks out and protests.*

Hanson (*to* **McQueen**)   You're walking on very thin ice.

McQueen (*trying to spit the blood away from his mouth*)   Is he annoyed because she has to go elsewhere? (*To* **Ellis**.) Are you? Is that what this is all about?

Hanson (*shaking his head*)   Oh, you think this is normal, huh? So we're over-reacting are we? I tell you what, let's go outside and drag someone in off the street . . . some bloke . . . bring him in here, tell him some fancy dan's dicking his wife for money. D'ya think he'd be happy about it?

McQueen   If he knew . . . if he thought about it.

Jarrett (*to* **Hanson**)   I know what we said, Richie, but this guy's getting on my tits.

McQueen   Oh, you're gonna torture some confession out of me . . . I'm gonna plead for my life . . . break down and –

Jarrett   See, I told you.

Ellis   They're all the same, butter wouldn't melt –

Hanson (*to* **Jarrett**)   You know what we agreed. I want answers . . . I wanna know why Shelly said she was going out to play bridge every Tuesday night . . . having girls' nights out with the coffee-morning crowd . . . learning to play badminton on Sunday nights. I wanna know why my credit card paid for a cigarette case with someone else's fucking initials on it. When I know and when I'm satisfied, then we can fuck this bastard over like he's fucked us over.

Ellis   Fucking A.

McQueen (*to* **Hanson**)   Are you the leader, then? Or is this a democracy?

Hanson   So why, Richard Gere, is my wife buying you presents and booking hotel rooms? Why is she lying to me?

McQueen   You really wanna know? All of you, huh?

Jarrett   That's why we're here.

McQueen   No tantrums, no fists, no weapons? Can you take it . . . the truth? It's not pleasant.

Hanson   No, it's not.

McQueen   It's very simple and it's all around us . . . this town stinks of it, this small-minded town where the women make the tea and keep the bed warm.

Ellis   What the f –

McQueen   You said you wanted to hear the truth. God knows, you won't like it . . . I know that, that's why I try and be discreet, but the simple fact is . . . is that your women, this town's women, want something else. They want to be valued, respected, loved and wanted. They want to feel wanted, gentlemen. And that, my friends, is it in a nutshell.

Silence for a few moments as it sinks in.

Ellis   You make them feel wanted?

McQueen   I make them feel special . . . I let them be someone else, somewhere else for as long as it takes. It's a service.

Jarrett (*shaking head*)   I don't believe this. You're shitting me . . . shitting all of us.

McQueen   Am I? Why?

Ellis   My wife . . . we . . . we love each other. We . . . don't bullshit me. My wife loves me.

McQueen   No one's disputing that.

Jarrett   Then what are you talking about? Huh? Fucking respect and . . . and feeling special and . . . how can you sit there, some . . . some ponce in a cheap suit, and tell me about my wife? I should fucking kill you . . . you . . .

Ellis (*to* **Hanson**)   He's taking the piss out of us, laughing at us. Look at him . . . look at his face, he's loving it. He thinks he's got something over us.

Hanson (*to* **McQueen**)   Is that right? 'S that what you think? D'you think you're superior because you can charge frustrated women fifty quid an hour or whatever it is and then pork them while their husband's at home watching the clock? 'S that . . . that it, Mr Smooth motherfucker? . . .

Suddenly, just as we think **Hanson***'s the cool, calm one, he lunges out and cuts* **McQueen***'s other cheek.* **McQueen** *shrieks out again, kicks out at his tormenters, who laugh at him.*

Ellis   Who's laughing now, eh?

They all laugh and high-five.

Jarrett   Piece of shit. You wanna take his fucking trousers off and cut the thing off. Let's see how many phone calls he gets then.

They all laugh again.

There is silence for a few moments for pause and recollection. **Ellis** *raids a small fridge beside the bedside table and retrieves some miniatures. He tosses one each to his friends and downs one himself. They all drink.*

Hanson (*to* **McQueen**)   How long you been seeing Shelly?

No answer. **McQueen** *is groggy.* **Hanson** *kicks his legs.*

Hanson   How long?

McQueen (*after a few moments*)   Six months.

Jarrett   And Janice?

McQueen   Same.

Ellis   My Sue?

McQueen   Bit less.

Hanson   Oh, I see a pattern here. It seems that one of our bored, unloved, unrespected wives got a tip-off here, then tipped off the other two bored, unloved, unrespected wives. And then I suppose the whole fucking bridge club got the nod. What about all the other women in the street? You must be one busy son of a bitch.

Jarrett   How did it all start?

McQueen   I dunno.

Jarrett   Try very hard.

McQueen   I . . . I got a call. Someone passed on my name. I'm registered, for Chrissakes. It's a fucking business.

Ellis   Oh, this gets better.

Hanson   A business? You have accounts . . . taxes . . . medical bills?

McQueen   I'm one in a thousand. It's not unique. It's a service . . . like I've been saying. I'm not out to hurt anyone. I'm not out to break up marriages, I'm . . . I'm there to save them.

Ellis *runs forward as if to hit him.* **Hanson** *steps in and holds him off.* **Ellis** *protests but backs away.*

Hanson   Save them?

McQueen   They talk to me. I listen to them . . . sometimes they fall asleep as they talk, they've so much to get off their chest. They talk, then they go home and their . . . their anger's gone . . . their frustrations have gone. They can be a wife again.

Jarrett   You talk after you've porked them. Is that it? Big wow.

McQueen   It's not all about sex. Sometimes we don't even have sex.

Ellis   So you're what . . . a counsellor, a listener, a great fuck, an all-round good guy? (*Sarcastic.*) Shit, I wish I could be like that.

Jarrett (*to* **Ellis**)   You know, what amazes me, this guy has no . . . and I mean no shame. He sits there talking about our wives . . . our great loves, the girls we've known for years and he's telling us the score.

McQueen   I'm telling you because you asked me. I could walk out of here, back to my wife and –

Ellis   This guy's from Jackanory –

McQueen (*ignoring him*)   – family and pick up where I left off. I was . . . am a carpenter, a damned good one, made plenty of money, but I wasn't happy. I started this and I can't stop. There's times when I wanted to, but you know what stopped me?

Ellis   Surprise us?

McQueen   The clients. They need me, and I need them. We're friends . . . real friends . . . we connect. I like them,

I look forward to seeing them. I look forward to sitting up with them all night talking about books and art and theatre. Don't you see, its what they want to hear. They want to hear it from you, but you can't . . . won't give it to them. I am you . . . that's all it is. I am each and every one of you standing in here. Wives don't want to talk about *Coronation Street* and drink a port and lemon at nine o'clock. They don't want to talk about egg and chips and two weeks in Benidorm. They want something else and that's what I give them. Yes, I give them sex, but I give them passion and I give them my heart.

Ellis I'm not buying any of this shit. (*To* **Hanson** *and* **Jarrett**.) Can't you see what he's doing . . . he's trying to turn it round and make us look like the villains. You can't believe what he's saying. If he's married, I'm a fucking magician.

McQueen I am married. Take a look.

He motions for **Ellis** *to check out his inside jacket pocket.* **Ellis** *stays rooted to the spot for some moments, unsure of what to do, feeling humiliated. He then moves forward, roots through jacket.* **McQueen** *regards him cockily, speaks sarcastically.*

McQueen That's right . . . left pocket. You got it . . .

Ellis *fishes out a wallet and brings out a photograph, which he regards then shows to his comrades.*

Ellis And she puts up with this?

McQueen It's a business . . . are you fucking deaf? It feeds her and the kids.

Ellis (*stuffing photo inside his crotch, rubbing it*) And do you stuff her after you've stuffed your clients? Does she get off on all this dodgy shit? Do you shower after or does she like to see your work?

McQueen *ignores him, motions for the return of the photo.* **Ellis** *regards it for a few moments longer, then rips it into tiny pieces.*

McQueen She's right about you.

Ellis (*incredulous*)   What? (*Approaching him.*) What did you say to me, you little prick?

McQueen   I said we talked, didn't I?

Ellis (*inches from* **McQueen**'s *face*)   You talk about me? Who do you think you are? (*Turns to comrades.*) Are you listening to this? (*Turns back.*) Have a good laugh at me, do you? Does it keep it up for you, does it? Feel superior do you? (*Turns to comrades.*) Are you two listening to this? Are you gonna let him talk to us like this?

Hanson   Whaddya wanna do?

Ellis (*walking towards him*)   You know what I wanna do.

Hanson (*to* **Jarrett**)   You?

Jarrett (*swigging whisky miniature*)   I wanna torture him . . . but hey, that's just me. (*Drinks again.*)

McQueen (*suddenly becoming worried*)   Hey, come on, you asked me? I . . . I didn't have to say a thing.

Ellis   You said too much.

McQueen   I said we talked.

Jarrett   Look, dickhead, you're not here to enjoy yourself.

McQueen   Does it look like I'm enjoying myself?

Jarrett   Actually, yeah . . . I see the way your lip curls when you talk and frankly it's getting on my tits.

McQueen   I mean, what do you want me to say? Shit, you know why I'm here, I can't deny that. I've tried to . . . to co-operate with you. I've tried to say it's not just sex.

Ellis   And that makes us all feel tip top, that does.

Hanson   Well, I reckon we've got plenty of time before Shelly turns up for her rogering or whatever the fuck she wants to do tonight. (*Sarcastic, looking at* **McQueen**.) You never know, she might wanna talk about the new fucking Jackson Pollock exhibition. Shit, she might wanna talk about me . . . might want her toes sucked. I don't have a clue any more. Anyway, we gotta decide what we're gonna do.

McQueen *shifts uneasily in his seat as* **Ellis** *picks up the bowie knife from the dressing table and fingers it deliciously.*

Ellis   Let's finish him.

Hanson   I'm gonna be waiting for her when she gets here, that's all I'm interested in.

McQueen (*frightened*)   I'll finish it if you want . . . if that's what you want. I can go back to . . . I can carve some wood again . . . that's fine with me.

Ellis   Until some hot totty finds your number and calls you at midnight. I bet that decision'll take all of three seconds.

McQueen   I'll quit the area . . . really. No sweat.

Jarrett (*circling him*)   Sorry, don't believe you. You're a liar, a creep and a fucking leech. Nothing but a two-bit cheap prostitute. You should be hanging on street corners and flagging down cars. Do you know what happens in this country when a prostitute is murdered? Huh? Do you?

McQueen   I –

Jarrett (*shouting*)   NOTHING. Fucking zilch. Nothing happens because nobody gives a flying fuck about them because they are the scum of the earth . . . the lowest of the low. Those fuckers will drop their pants for ten quid and a drive home. They stick their veins full of shit, spread disease all over the stinking country and they want tolerance.

McQueen   You're wrong. You –

Jarrett   'S like the Ripper. He killed a load of prostitutes and nobody gave a fuck, but the moment he slipped up and killed an innocent, everyone was up in arms. The police are working a hundred-hour week and the papers are full of warnings. Because a person has been killed . . . a person, not a drain on society. Not someone who wants and won't give. Am I making myself clear, pretty boy?

McQueen   Crystal.

Ellis   He doesn't care. I dunno why you're wasting your breath.

McQueen (*to* **Ellis**)   Oh I care, and that's what this is all about isn't it? I care, me . . . a leech. I care, and you . . . you, well, you know. You know. You know that I know all about you and that's why you've got a bee up your arse.

Ellis (*to* **Hanson**)   See what I mean.

Hanson *is leaning against the dressing table. He takes a swig from a miniature. He ignores the scene.*

Ellis (*to* **McQueen**, *sarcastic*)   Leave the country . . . give it all up? You might have to get your hands dirty.

McQueen   Let me ask you a simple question. Why do you think your wife comes to me? Simple question.

Ellis *stands centre stage, shifting from foot to foot. He looks at his comrades who sit drinking, leaving him alone to respond. He is clearly uncomfortable.*

Ellis   Because I work hard and I . . . I work late and

McQueen   No.

Ellis   Whaddya mean, 'no'?

McQueen   I heard you're a ditherer, Jed . . . a bit of a worrier. What's the name . . . your nickname . . . a bit of an irony, but she calls you Viagra because you're up all night. Not up, if you get my drift, but up fucking crying and moaning about your business, about the overheads . . . about the foreman. Yeah, Jimmy, she calls you Viagra. She calls me up and tells me Viagra's straining on the toilet . . . he can't shit either.

Ellis *stands centre stage unable to move. He can't believe what he is hearing. Suddenly,* **Jarrett** *bursts into laughter.*

Jarrett (*drinking*)   Viagra . . . can't keep it up.

Ellis *stands, tearful. He looks at* **Hanson** *for guidance, but he simply stands firm. He walks to* **Jarrett**, *who laughs at him.* **Ellis** *then paces the stage mumbling to himself whilst the room's occupants simply watch him. Finally he sits on a bed and wraps his hands round his head.*

Hanson (*to* **McQueen**)   Congratulations. It's not enough that he has to hear about his wife fucking a gigolo. No, he has to be humiliated in front of his friends.

McQueen   He needs to know. You all need to know. He thinks his wife's a possession and I took it like taking a car out of his garage. It's the same anger. His wife needs sex. She loves him, sure she does. She worships the ground he walks on, but she needs the –

Suddenly **Ellis** *rises and lets out a bloodcurdling, defiant roar. He stands there eyeing the three of them, his tears falling freely, feeling utterly broken. He lunges towards* **McQueen** *and makes as though to stab him through the heart with the knife he holds. It is a tense moment.* **Ellis** *stands, the knife hovering close to* **McQueen**'s *chest. His hand starts to tremble. He drops the knife and lets out another tortured roar. He turns to face* **Jarrett**, *who moves towards him, apologising.* **Ellis** *knocks him away, drops knife and exits through door, running. There is silence for a few moments.* **Hanson** *sits on bed opposite* **McQueen**, *and* **Jarrett** *raids the fridge again.* **Hanson** *declines a drink, so* **Jarrett** *drinks, sitting on the other bed.*

Hanson   Clock's ticking fast.

McQueen   And?

Hanson   You'll see.

McQueen   You gonna have it out with your wife? You gonna kill her?

Hanson   That doesn't concern you. You won't be seeing her again, anyway.

Jarrett   True.

McQueen (*to* **Jarrett**)   You're an interesting character.

Jarrett   What the fuck? Oh, is it time for my psychoanalysis now, is it? Are you gonna fuck with my head now?

McQueen   Well, if it's confession time tonight . . . if it's truth you want . . . if it's truth we all want, then why not? It's why you're here. 'S what you said. It was the first question . . . 'Why are you fucking my wife?'

Jarrett   My wife's dead. She's lying in the bath at home with a shower-cord wrapped round her neck. S'funny, but I thought you knew that . . . thought Richie told you when you first sat down.

McQueen   Okay, why did I fuck your wife?

Jarrett   That's better.

McQueen   You wanna know?

Jarrett   If it'll help you. Personally, I couldn't give a shit, but it seems to make your balls grow a bit bigger.

McQueen   You're gonna enjoy this. When you look into my eyes as you cut my throat, you're gonna see it in my eyes. You're gonna watch me smile because I knew all along and –

Jarrett   Okay, cut the melodrama. Jesus, you love listening to your own voice, don't ya?

Hanson   Too much.

McQueen   Your wife. I like her . . . sorry, liked her. I honestly think she was the best of the bunch. She was the sensitive one, the real sweetie. But . . . and this isn't easy, she . . . well, let me ask you. Remember that time she said she had to go to the doctor's . . . the first time, what, about four, five months ago. You remember?

Jarrett   Yeah. So?

McQueen   What was it, headaches, migraine . . . something or other. The doc gave her a sackload of pills and she takes them and now she's feeling okay apart from the odd twinge, right?

Jarrett (*tentative*)   Right.

McQueen   That is right, isn't it?

Jarrett   Yes, yes, that's right. She gets a migraine, what's new?

McQueen   Gets?

Jarrett   What?

McQueen   Gets? You said gets. Don't you mean got? I thought she was dead.

Jarrett (*confused*)   Gets, got . . . whatever . . .

McQueen   Well your *dead* wife didn't have headaches, Mr Jarrett, no I'm afraid it was a tad more serious that that.

Jarrett (*pausing mid-drink*)   Fucking doctor as well as counsellor. Shit, you're wasted, you are.

McQueen (*shaking head*)   Your wife . . . your wife, Mr Jarrett, has cancer . . .

Silence descends like a cloud. **Hanson** *shifts uneasily and decides to take a drink.* **Jarrett** *rises and moves closer to* **McQueen**.

Jarrett   I'm sorry . . . (*He yanks his hair back and forces his mouth open. Pours in whisky.*) I'm sorry, what was that?

McQueen *coughs, splutters, gargles and kicks out.* **Hanson** *rises and pulls* **Jarrett** *back, forcing him away.* **Jarrett** *sits back down, then abruptly rises again and charges* **McQueen**, *who continues to struggle and splutter.* **Hanson** *stops* **Jarrett** *mid-punch and forces him to sit down under protest.*

Jarrett   You heard what he said?

Hanson   I heard.

Jarrett   Some fucking gigolo who thinks he's Jesus. As if I wouldn't know my wife has cancer. She gets headaches, for Chrissakes.

Hanson   I know, man.

Jarrett   Look at him, fucking smiling and laying the law down.

McQueen   I'm telling the truth. You know it, that's why you're so angry. You know it.

Jarrett *tries to lunge again but is stopped by* **Hanson**.

McQueen   It's the same with her . . . anger . . . confusion. You can't talk to her. How could she tell you something like that?

Hanson   I think that's enough.

McQueen   He has to know. He hasn't killed his wife. He hasn't got the balls. He's a big man with a knife and a friend. It takes balls to talk to your wife.

Jarrett *manages to get hold of* **McQueen** *and to get a few punches in.* **Hanson** *holds back. After a few moments of pummelling which leaves* **McQueen** *bloodied,* **Jarrett** *spits on him, then staggers back and reaches for another miniature. Suddenly* **McQueen** *bursts into laughter and continues for some moments. Both men watch him incredulously.*

McQueen   And you wonder why your wife couldn't talk to you? There's no love in your heart, just pride and sloth. You can split my skull open but you can never rid my mind of what I know . . . what I see. I am here . . . I am put on this earth to protect women from people like you. Hey, do you think one of those blows to the head when you were pissed . . . do you think mebbe one of those punches might've caused the imbalance? It's possible.

Jarrett   I didn't hit anyone . . . especially my wife. You're a liar.

McQueen   Then why wouldn't she tell you? Tell me that.

Hanson (*to* **McQueen**)   You're not helping. This is spite.

McQueen   Well, you fucking sit here and let me beat your head in and fuck with your mind. I'm telling this prick because he should know.

Hanson   He's gonna kill you.

McQueen   I know. But then, when I'm dead, who's gonna tell him about Janice?

Jarrett   She has not got fucking cancer. I would know.

McQueen   I sit there with her, her head on my lap. She cries as she tells me. She's frightened, oh shit she's frightened . . . mainly for her parents and the baby. But she's also frightened because she can't tell you . . . doesn't want to. You see, you have to care about someone to tell them something like that . . . have to trust them. She doesn't love you, Jarrett, and that's why she won't tell you. She's not trying to spare your feelings. She wants you to be the last to know. She wants you to feel guilty . . . to feel pain like she's felt it every day for five years. She wants you to wake up one morning next to her and find her dead. And do you know what, she'll have a big smile on her face, because she'll be free.

Jarrett   I don't believe you.

McQueen   Course you don't. You don't want to, it hurts your ego, doesn't it? This is what this is all about. You don't give a fuck about your wife. You don't ask where she goes when she has to visit the hospital twice a week.

Jarrett   This is all . . . (*Swigs whisky.*) . . . all bollocks.

McQueen   She cries herself to sleep. I listen to her pour it all out. I stroke her hair and I tell her she's beautiful. Have you told her she's beautiful, huh? Have you?

Jarrett (*to* **Hanson**)   Are you listening to this, Richie . . . you're next, man. He's fucked Jed's mind, now he's pushing me over. How can you sit there and listen to this?

Hanson (*slight pause*)   'Cause its true.

Jarrett (*incredulous*)   What?

Hanson   She's ill man, I know. I . . . I thought you knew. Obviously I thought you knew.

Jarrett   What, and you think I wouldn't've mentioned it in passing?

Hanson   Well, I dunno, some people act in different ways y'know. Sure I thought it was strange, but --

Jarrett   Every fucker knows but me, eh? You've let this twat rabbit on here, you've let me deny it . . . fucking ridicule it, and it's true. What sort of mate are you?

Hanson   It wasn't my place.

Jarrett (*rising, shaking head*)   No. I dunno what the hell's happened here tonight, but we've ended up being . . . being given a morality lesson by some tart with a heart. What happened to the big picture, Richie? Huh? Did we leave our balls inside the wardrobes?

Hanson   You've got your own mind.

Jarrett (*approaching* **Hanson**)   Hey, you're the one who put this together . . . you're the one who wanted to even the score.

Hanson   I wanted answers.

Jarrett   Shit, we've got 'em, haven't we? We've got one guy on his way home with his tail between his legs and one step away from a psychiatric ward and I've been told my wife's dying by Champagne Charlie here. And . . . and . . . hold the phone . . . everybody else knows about it. (*Sits back down in despair.*)

Hanson   So where's your balls? Instead of marinating yourself in whisky, why don't you do it? Why don't you do what you've been planning all week?

Jarrett   Fuck you.

Hanson (*angry*)   No, Jamie, fuck you. I'm sick of holding your hand all the time. You want action, you take it.

Jarrett   I bet you feel really good, eh? I mean, where's the mud that sticks to you, eh? Can't you see the picture? One down, another one halfway down . . . soon it's gonna be your turn. Then what's gonna happen, eh? You're gonna have to listen to some home truths. Only thing is, you won't have an audience. You won't have to squirm. (*Turns to* **McQueen**.) So what about it, pretty boy? Enjoying this, eh? What's in store for our leader, then?

McQueen   We'll see.

Jarrett   I'm sure we will. Why talk in sentences when a riddle'll do, eh? (*To* **Hanson**.) Hey Richie, y'know what, something's just dawned on me . . . just thought how neat this is, like one of those old films . . . seems like a set-up. Have you got something going with this bloke? Is he blowing you off for fifty quid an hour? Does he stroke your hair till you fall asleep?

Hanson   I'm starting to wonder.

McQueen   Hey, I'm no fag.

Hanson   No, I'm starting to wonder . . . starting to see things a bit clearer as well. You think you know people . . . think you know what makes people tick and –

Jarrett   You think too much.

Hanson   I've stood here all night and heard you bellyache about this and that. All the time when this guy told you how much of a shit you were to Janice, you never said, 'No, I love my wife' . . . you only responded to your pride . . . your wounded pride. This guy's right.

Jarrett   Then stick that bowie knife in my back . . . a second time.

Hanson   He's right about me . . . about you and Ellis. He's right about everything. When did you tell Janice you loved her?

Jarrett   I don't know.

Hanson   This month, this year . . . ever?

Jarrett   What about you? What about Mr Perfect here? Your missus is never at home. She's with this bloke more than any of 'em put together.

Hanson   He's fucking right and that turns me inside out to admit it. I've been listening to this . . . all this shit tonight and I've been listening to myself. Look at his face . . . I carved his cheek. Yeah, okay, I wanted to put him on a meat hook because he made me look a fool. Yeah, he fucked my wife. Yeah, she probably screamed this fucking motel down, but he hurt my pride. That's the crux. He said it himself. He took something of mine.

Jarrett   And he should pay.

McQueen (*tentative*)   Don't you think . . . don't you think I've learned something from this?

Jarrett   Hey, mister, just . . . just button it, will you?

McQueen   No, please. You were . . . you were guys in my head. There were no faces, no flesh to the bones. I see you now. I hear you . . . really listened to you (*Points to* **Hanson**.) and that doesn't make me feel good. I don't take satisfaction from hurting you and I apologise to you – (*Points to* **Jarrett**.) – for saying what I said, but I . . . I see the way women are treated and –

Jarrett   Yeah, we get the message Gandhi and I'm pig-sick of it. (*To* **Hanson**.) I never thought I'd see the day when I heard you agreeing with this prick.

Hanson   Well, sometimes you have to look at yourself.

Jarrett   So do it.

Hanson   Oh, I have.

Jarrett   Not hard enough.

Hanson   Sometimes it just goes a little bit deeper.

Jarrett   Doesn't it just?

Hanson   You're not the only one who's lost here tonight.

Jarrett   Hey, I haven't lost anything, mate. It seems like I never had anything.

Hanson   I think you did . . . you still do.

Jarrett   Well at least you've still got yours and you've gained a pal. This guy's a smart cookie, mebbe you should hire him. For someone who was gonna have the balls of a field mouse, he certainly taught you something. Mebbe he should run your business, leave you with a bit of time with your wife.

Hanson   You know he's right, but I know you can't admit it. That's fine.

Jarrett   Oh, is that it? Is that the cue to go? Have we reached stalemate now?

Hanson   We had no intention of killing him, you know that. He fucking knows that . . . he knows, man. We were here to shake him up, put the frighteners on him, make sure he didn't do it again. Sure, we'd hurt him but that'd be enough, he'd learn his lesson. We'd strip him, beat him, turn him out onto the street with his final warning and that would be enough. We'd be vindicated, our job done. No more phone calls. No more after-hours servicing and no more deception. That's what all this was about. You know that.

Jarrett   And I go home and go back to my wife who hates me?

McQueen   Hey, maybe I was a bit –

Jarrett (*holding out his hands in warding-off gesture, turns to* **Hanson**)   I go back to her and we live happily ever after?

Hanson   Why not?

Jarrett   And what about her . . . what about the illness? What, do I just forget about it? Do I let her go on seeing him?

McQueen   I won't –

Jarrett (*shouting*)   I TOLD YOU TO SHUT THE FUCK UP . . . DO YOU HEAR ME? I DON'T WANNA HEAR YOUR VOICE AGAIN AND I DON'T EVER WANNA SEE YOUR FACE AGAIN. IS THAT CLEAR? IS IT?

McQueen *nods.*

Jarrett   By God, it'd better be. (*To* **Hanson**.) How do I know about it . . . the illness?

Hanson   We had a beer, I let it slip.

Jarrett   And him?

Hanson   He won't see her again. He's retired. There's a need for good carpenters around here.

Jarrett   And I'll . . . I'll – (*Frustration bursts out finally and he breaks down.*) – tell her I love her?

Hanson (*arm around* **Jarrett**)   She knows. Deep down . . . where it matters.

Jarrett   I love her so much it hurts. That's why I'm here. (*Still crying.*) He's wrong, it's . . . it's not about possessions, it's about my life. She is my life . . . she . . .

McQueen *goes to speak.* **Hanson** *shakes his head at him.* **Hanson** *comforts* **Jarrett** *until the lights fade slowly. A light focuses on* **Hanson** *and* **Jarrett** *for some moments, then fades to blackout.*

Act Two

Lights rise again in same motel room. Some attempt has been made to return the room to order. Only two people are now present. **McQueen** *stands beside the dressing table, dabbing at his cuts with a towel and wringing his stiff hands.* **Hanson** *sits on a chair.*

Hanson So, why didn't I get the humiliation . . . the ordeal? Or are you sparing my feelings?

McQueen (*tentative, sits on bed*) Shelly's . . . Shelly's different?

Hanson Different?

McQueen She's . . . er . . . she's a predator.

Hanson (*sarcastic*) That's my girl.

McQueen No, really . . . I . . . listen, this is difficult for me. I wanna be straight with you . . . okay?

Hanson Sure.

McQueen I don't like her. She frightens me. She . . . she treats me like . . . like I'm some sort of slave, like I only work for her and I should be at her beck and call.

Hanson And this isn't part of the . . . the *job*?

McQueen She won't take no for an answer. The other clients, they . . . they understand that I have a life. They know I'm married, that I love my wife and kids, but Shelly, she . . . she's trying to fuck it up.

Hanson Fuck it up? How?

McQueen She wouldn't believe I was serious about my family. She teases me . . . tells me that we were meant to be together . . . tells me my family are in the past . . . that she's the future. I'm being straight with you, Mr Hanson. I love my job, but I love my wife and family more than anything.

Hanson And you're saying my wife . . . my wife, who wouldn't say boo to a goose, is some sort of maniac? Is that what you're telling me?

McQueen   I know it's hard –

Hanson   Do you? Do you really? It's one thing telling me you're poking her cause she's bored, but it's another story telling me she's trying to wreck two families.

McQueen   I'm trying to be straight with you. You should know what she's like.

Hanson   I don't think I wanna know.

McQueen   You've gotta help me stop this.

Hanson (*incredulous*)   I have to help you! How'd'ya work that out?

McQueen   Because she's sick . . . she's . . . I tell you, man, she's frightening me. I don't know what's gonna happen next.

Hanson   So why keep meeting her?

McQueen   I have to.

Hanson   I thought you –

McQueen   I mean, I have to . . . I mean she makes me. She's got a hold over me and she's strangling me with it. Every time the phone rings I jump. My kids are wondering why their daddy's grumpy all the time and they're sick of him and Mammy screaming at each other all the time. I tell you, this woman's making me ill.

Hanson   And do you . . . do you fuck her every time?

McQueen (*slight pause for recollection*)   Yeah, but it's not just sex . . . it's not making love . . . it's not passion. It's pain, it's hard and it's seedy. You complain about the motel, it's all part of the game. It's about control, about opposites. It's about cursing you while I fuck her up the arse and –

Hanson   Hey, I get the fucking message.

McQueen   Do you think I enjoy talking like this? Huh? Look at me (*Raises a hand to show that he is shaking.*) I'm a nervous wreck. This is not why I came into this business. I told you why. It's about women like Janice and Susie

Ellis . . . loving women who need a shoulder. I don't need women like her.

Hanson   Then bin her . . . be a man, stop acting like a fucking pussy.

McQueen (*laughs in desperation*)   Oh sure. Have you been listening to anything I've been saying? Do you think I'm getting off on this?

Hanson   How the hell do I know? You're talking about some other woman . . . this, all this is alien to me.

McQueen   Then listen.

Hanson   What?

McQueen   When she finally shows up.

Hanson   Are you crazy? Listen to you?

McQueen   Not like that. I mean, listen to what she says to me. Then you'll know. Just spend a few minutes inside the wardrobe and you'll hear it all without fail.

Hanson (*incredulous*)   Spy on her? A fucking voyeur? How do I know this isn't some game?

McQueen   You'll see. You'll know straight away.

Hanson   I dunno, I –

McQueen (*goading him*)   You have to see . . . you have to find out what she's really like. You're the only one who can stop it.

Hanson   It doesn't sound like it, the way she's coming across.

McQueen   She won't listen to me, but she'd be devastated if you knew.

Hanson   Why's that? What difference would it make?

McQueen   The game'd be over. It's her fantasy.. her very oxygen. She needs this deceit . . . this . . . this power. If you knew, it'd break it down the middle, get to the root of it all.

Hanson (*shaking head, throwing up arms*)   I tell you, this is all way over my head.

McQueen   She phones me from work . . . she phones me from the toilet . . . phones me whilst you lay asleep next to her. She loves it . . . it fuels her.

Hanson   While I'm asleep?

McQueen   She takes the piss, tells me you lasted forty seconds and –

Hanson (*rising, angry*)   Watch your mouth.

McQueen   Okay, okay. I'm sorry man, but you have to know. You have to help –

Hanson   Help you?

McQueen   Mebbe . . . but yourself . . . her. She's gonna blow, I tell you. If I reject her she's gonna blow. I have to keep on seeing her because of that fear, and she feeds on that like a fucking vampire.

Hanson   So where is she now if she can't wait to use you?

McQueen   Oh, she'll be hanging about in some bar, letting men drool over her. She might even let a couple kiss her, get her ready. All part of the big picture. She knows I'll be here, pacing the floor, wondering what the fuck's gonna happen tonight.

Hanson (*pacing floor, incredulous*)   She hangs around in bars . . . she trawls. I can't . . . I don't fucking believe this.

McQueen   Listen man, you've gotta believe me. I'm not doing this out of spite or hatred or whatever. I need your help.

Hanson *ignores him. He paces floor for a few more moments and goes to fridge and takes out a couple of bottles which he downs in one. He leans against wall and stares at* **McQueen**.

Hanson   My life's crashing all around me and you want my help. You fucking started all this shit and you want my help? You leave two of my friends like gibbering idiots, tell

me my wife likes it up the arse and you want my help?
Fucking poetic.

McQueen   I didn't know it was gonna turn out like this.

Hanson   Oh well, what a shame. Somebody shoulda told
you it would be all sweetness and light, shouldn't they?
Shoulda told you it was all leg-over and no comeback. How
many lives you've ruined and you're frightened of a little
responsibility. Fuck you.

McQueen   No. I'm not frightened of responsibility, I'm
frightened of the consequences. I'm frightened about my
parents, my wife and my children.

Hanson   Oh, give me a break.

McQueen   Yeah, I'll give you a break. I'll give you a
break after you've stood in that wardrobe and heard your
dear wife. And you can cut me from facecheek to arsecheek
if you want, but it is your responsibility to listen. You can
fillet me and serve me to your mates, but I won't have my
family fucked over this.

Hanson (*cynical*)   Your parents? What, has she asked for a
foursome?

McQueen   No. She found it in herself to send some
anonymous photos to them, to scare the shit outta a coupla
sixty-year-olds. Is that right? Is that part of the big picture?

Hanson   Hey, I never said it was.

McQueen   She followed my wife into a supermarket once,
bumped into her and slipped some bottles into her overcoat
right under the closed-circuit. Luckily my wife cottoned on
'cause they weighed her down, but that wasn't Shelly's
concern. She didn't even want my wife to get caught, she
just wanted her to know . . . to know that she could fuck
with her like she fucks with me. Simple. She's ran her off
the road, rings her up maybe twenny, thirty times a day –

Hanson   Shit, this is all Scully and Mulder territory. I
don't –

McQueen   She picked my kids up from school one day . . .
must've been watching that shit movie with Michael Douglas,
and she drove them around the town for a few hours, knowing full well that myself and my wife would be shitting bricks,
but she also knew we wouldn't call the police. I mean, what
are we gonna say . . . 'Sorry, officer, this loony's carted our
kids off because my secret, paid-for liaisons with her aren't
enough for her and she wants a little bit more.' Oh yeah, I can
see that one. I can see the coppers losing sleep over that one.

Hanson   Does the term 'We reap what we sow' mean
anything to you?

McQueen   Oh, I deserve it?

Hanson   Maybe.

McQueen   But do my wife and kids? Is it justice to call
two of my clients and tell them I've got AIDS and I'm
spreading it 'cause I'm pissed off with society? Do those
women deserve it? Do their families? Can you imagine what
it was like for them waiting for the results? Can you?

Hanson *remains impassive.*

McQueen   The bottom line, and this is where it's all
coming back to, is – do you care?

Hanson   Maybe, maybe not. Maybe all this has left me
with one option.

McQueen   Which is?

Hanson   To sail off into the sunset and let you and your
sordid little world drown in all the shit and slime it trawls
around in.

McQueen   Eloquent.

Hanson   Well I don't feel eloquent. I don't feel good.
I don't feel justified or satisfied. I feel sick . . . sick to my
stomach of all this . . . this decay I see around me . . . all
the decadence I've heard . . . all the lies, the deceit . . . the
hatred. You may be schooled in it, Mr McQueen, but its
taking me a bit of time to come to terms with.

McQueen   But it didn't have to be like this . . . doesn't have to be like this.

Hanson   One bad apple, huh? And that bad apple eats my food, drives my second car and warms my frozen dinners. Christ, what a fuck-up.

McQueen   I . . . I keep thinking that one day a body's gonna turn up floating in a river or something with my semen inside her . . . or they're gonna find my fingerprints at a murder scene. She's even threatened to kill me.

Hanson (*cynical*)   What with, her handbag?

McQueen   She's got a gun.

Hanson (*incredulous*)   What?

McQueen   I've seen it. All part –

Hanson   – of the game . . . yeah, yeah, I fucking heard it already.

McQueen   Are you listening to me? She's threatened to kill me.

Hanson   Isn't that part of the sex?

McQueen   I'm serious. She's pulled it on me before and she's not bluffing. I can see it in her eyes. I woke during the night and she was sitting on top of me with the gun pressed against my mouth. And she was laughing. She said if I left her she'd kill me first, then my family, then herself.

Hanson   And I thought my life sucked.

McQueen   She's reversed the roles. In your life you're the dominant one. She does what you ask, would never disagree . . . you're in control. She respects you . . . fears you. Now she wants to feel that, so she's doing it with me. She's hurting you by using your money and she also wants your anger, your energy. She's got it, Mr Hanson, and by Christ she doesn't wanna lose it.

Hanson   Then do me a favour and deal with it. I've had enough of this shit. I'm tired, bored and my head's been fucked with too much. If my wife shows up tell her this is her last rendezvous and –

McQueen (*agitated*)   What . . . what, you're not going. I thought . . . thought you were gonna help me?

Hanson (*rising*)   Who said that?

McQueen   But I . . . you can't . . . didn't you listen to what I said? Huh? She's a –

Hanson   Listen, mate, I heard you tear my two pals to bits, but you're not gonna do the same to me. I've been waiting here for Shelly to show up and prove that something's going on and I'm still here. Mebbe you're a bit self-delusional or mebbe some of that hair gel's seeped into your brain and dulled your senses.

McQueen   No, she's playing with me . . . I told you. She probably knows you're here. She's probably waiting for you to leave, then –

Hanson   Fuck this bollocks. I've waited and now I'm going. I waited for my wife to turn up cause it's written in her diary. I wanted to find you two together and . . . and . . . it doesn't matter now.

McQueen (*desperate*)   No, please, you can't go.

Hanson *drains the last of his whisky and walks to window, looks out, shakes his head and makes to walk towards door.* **McQueen** *rises quickly and blocks his path.*

Hanson   I'm not in the mood for any more of this bullshit.

McQueen (*clearly frightened*)   No, I'm begging you. You cannot leave. You have to see what she's like. Okay . . . okay, you don't believe me, so wait and listen. That's all I ask.

Hanson   Get out of my way. You don't wanna tangle with me now. I'm tired and my head aches. Now get the fuck away from me.

Hanson *brushes past him and makes for the door. He turns the knob.* **McQueen** *rushed towards him and spins him round. He holds the bowie knife in his hand.*

McQueen (*desperate*)   I'm desperate. I don't want to use this but I will. I'm desperate for your help. Sit down, please. She might've tried to phone but you smashed my mobile. She might've tried to tell me she'll be late. Please sit.

Hanson *stands near door, rubbing his temples, saying nothing. He stands on spot, staring at* **McQueen**.

McQueen   Come over here and sit down.

Hanson *walks towards fridge, brings out a beer, walks towards bed, away from his adversary and sits drinking in silence.* **McQueen** *walks towards the window, his eyes still trained on* **Hanson**. **McQueen** *is agitated; shaking and mumbling. He pulls curtain back slightly and takes a few curious glances out. He then turns back to* **Hanson** *who has turned his back on him.*

McQueen (*leaning against window frame*)   I . . . I just want you to hear . . . then you'll know.

He continues to take peeks out of the window as **Hanson** *drinks, remaining tight-lipped. There is an uneasy, truce-like silence for a few moments.* **McQueen** *goes to speak, then the phone breaks the silence.* **McQueen** *jumps.* **Hanson** *turns to him.* **McQueen** *checks him out, then the phone.*

Hanson   Well, I reckon that must be for you. Whaddya say?

McQueen *walks towards it, draws back, looks towards* **Hanson** *for guidance.*

Hanson   Or it could be management wondering what the noise's been about.

He laughs. Telephone continues to ring, then rings off. **McQueen** *stands, dazed, before it.*

Hanson   Or it could be my two pals, refreshed and ready to party. They could've brought the police. Me, I reckon it's my darling wife looking for Mr Goodbar.

Phone rings again.

McQueen *walks gingerly towards it and picks it up tentatively. He stands staring at* **Hanson**.

McQueen (*tentative*)   Hello? Shell? Hi . . . No, fine. No,
I was in the bathroom and I . . . Tired? Me . . . No, are
you kidding? Where've you been? I've been waiting a long
time, baby. You're gonna what . . . just a minute baby, room
service with the shampoo . . . just a second.

He motions **Hanson** *to come towards the phone and listen. After a
few agonising moments of wondering if he will,* **Hanson** *rises and
goes towards* **McQueen** *who holds out the phone.*

McQueen   Hey baby, give it to me again . . .

Hanson *listens as* **McQueen** *goads her into talking dirty. After
some moments of this,* **Hanson** *sits back down shaking his head.
He looks crushed.*

McQueen   How long you gonna be? Two minutes? I'm
ready, baby. Ready and willing. (*Puts phone down.*) I've got
two minutes. You gonna help me?

Hanson   I just heard.

McQueen   She's gotta know you heard. Okay, you know
I'm not shitting you, but she's got to know you're here. You
come outta that wardrobe after a few minutes and scare the
shit out of her. That'll be it. That's what she needs.

Hanson   And you'll go along with it?

McQueen   Whatever you want, man. Just please . . .
please get in there and come out when she gets too hot.

Hanson   But how do I know this isn't a set-up?

McQueen (*agitated*)   Oh shit, what do you want? She'll be
up the stairs, man.

Hanson   How do I know you're not gonna pile in and
stab me or whatever?

McQueen (*holds out knife*)   Here, take this. Your boy took
the holdall with all the gear in it . . . this's all that's left. I'm
not armed. You can frisk me man. Hurry up.

Hanson *takes the knife, puts it in his jacket pocket and then moves* *quickly to frisk* **McQueen**, *whom he finds is clean. There is a knock at the door.*

Hanson   You screw me and you're dead, and I'll make sure your family'll soon follow.

McQueen   I swear. Go, go.

Hanson *backs slowly away from him, watching him all the time, never turning his back on him. Finally he slips inside the wardrobe and pulls it closed after him, concealing him completely.* **McQueen** *pauses for a moment to regain his composure and notices empties on floor which he kicks under bed. Knocking rises in volume. He steps forwards and opens door.*

In breezes **Shelly Hanson** *a beautiful, confident young woman. She throws her coat at* **McQueen** *who catches it and puts it around chair. She shuts door with her high heeled shoe and walks centre-stage.* **McQueen** *follows her and they kiss passionately.* **Shelly** *breaks off, holds him outstretched with her hands. She regards him coyly.*

McQueen   What?

Shelly   What's that . . . on your face?

Goes to touch it, **McQueen** *winces.*

Shelly   It looks –

McQueen   Yesterday . . . some bastard jumped me . . . hit me with a knuckleduster or something. Some client's boyfriend who found out, I suppose. You should see his face. (*Laughs unconvincingly.*)

Shelly   My poor baby. Let Mammy kiss it better.

She moves towards him and kisses his face, mouth etc, allows her hands to wander over him, finally resting on his crotch.

Shelly   Oh Bobby, Mammy's offended. What's the matter with my baby? Why is he as soft as a baby's botty, huh?

McQueen (*tentative*)   I'm a . . . I'm a bit tense, that's all.

Shelly   Tense? I don't pay one hundred smackeroonies for tension.

McQueen   I know, baby, give me a bit of time, huh? I've never missed the spot yet, have I?

Shelly (*ignoring him, scouring room, backing away*)   So where's the champers, I'm dry.

McQueen   Oh, the guy knocked to say they ran out. There's a honeymoon suite along the lobby . . . lots of guests staying over as well, and you know what that means?

Shelly   What? My honeymoon night lasted about five minutes.

McQueen (*lying down on one of the beds*)   So why you so late?

Shelly   I got chatting.

McQueen   Oh yeah.

Shelly   Don't tell me you're jealous.

McQueen   Jealous . . . moi? I'm only the hired hand.

Shelly (*suddenly venomous*)   What the fuck is that supposed to mean?

McQueen (*shocked, sitting up*)   Nothing baby, I . . . you know, a joke.

Shelly   I don't pay you to joke.

McQueen   I know, but I like to talk. I like to know what you've been doing. I like to know who who've been talking to till – (*Checks watch.*) – ten past one.

Shelly   I've been talking to a man with the biggest dick I've ever seen in my life. (*Regards him closely.*) Well, second biggest. (*She bursts into laughter, sounding really cheap. She heads towards fridge, looks in.*) Jesus, Bobby, what the hell happened in here, you have a fucking party or something?

McQueen   They probably haven't checked it over since the last people were in here.

Shelly (*bringing out the rest of the alcohol and tossing it on bed. She joins him on his bed and takes a swig of vodka.*)   Happy to see me?

McQueen   What do you think?

Shelly   Dunno, that's why I'm asking.

McQueen   I'm always happy to see you . . . you're my
favourite –

Shelly (*putting her hand over his mouth*)   I hate liars.

McQueen   Who's lying?

Shelly   You don't wanna see me, spend time with me. I can
read you like a book.

McQueen   Course I wanna see you. You . . . you just get
a little heavy sometimes. I love spending time with you baby,
but you gotta give me some space. You've gotta let me have
my life back.

Shelly (*rising*)   Oh, fuck you. Fuck that shit. You'd leave
with me tomorrow if you weren't so moralistic. We can have
a great life but you keep up with this . . . this pretence
about your marriage and your picket fences and your –

McQueen   It's not pretence Shelly. *This* is pretence. We are
pretence. This is a deal . . . a deal between two consenting
adults who –

Shelly (*turning away from him, sits on end of bed and drinks*)   Yeah,
yeah. I've heard it all before. We both know it's a crock of
shit. We both know you're gonna wake up one morning and
know that this . . . what we have is real. You make love to
me like you do and you tell me it's not real. You lick me all
over . . . tell me you love me, and you're saying its an act.

McQueen   Yeah.

Shelly   Well, not to me it isn't.

McQueen   Jesus Christ, Shelly, I've told you a thousand
times.

*He reaches out for her, she smacks his hands away sharply. Silence for
a few moments.*

Shelly (*back to him, upset*)   I . . . I can't live like this. I . . .
I need you. This isn't enough. Seeing you for a few hours . . .
it's . . . it's tearing me apart.

McQueen   Then we have to end it now. We can be friends, we can enjoy each other, but this running away together stuff is fantasy. How many times do I have to tell you? How many times do you have to abuse my family?

Shelly   Till you submit.

McQueen *rises from bed, walks towards wardrobe, takes a tentative look, then walks towards window and looks out.* **Shelly** *still faces away from him. Silence for a few tense moments.*

McQueen   So, do you wanna make love?

Shelly   Love?

McQueen   Wanna fuck, then?

Shelly *(facing him)*   I've suddenly lost the mood. You stand there with my heart crushed under your boot and you talk so . . . so matter-of-fact. Do you know how much that hurts? You told me I was special. You're just a cheap fucking liar. You don't do this job because you care for women. I don't believe it. You can talk all you like. Talk's cheap. You do this job because you can fuck beautiful women and get paid for it and get women falling in love with you. That must make your hard-on extra special.

McQueen   Mebbe we should call it a night.

Shelly   No way. I've paid my fee. I bought this stinking room and I bought you.

McQueen *(grabbing chair, placing it dramatically centre stage, sitting, spreads out arms)*   Then tie me up, suck my cock and get out of here. This is just too much. I don't need this. If I wanted a mindfuck every day I'd join the Inland Revenue. *(He rises.)*

Shelly *(moving towards him, facing him)*   Don't speak to me like that. *(Slaps him, he winces.)*

McQueen   Hey, do me a favour and just leave will you.

Shelly   I'm going to sit here and decide how to spend my husband's well-earned dough. *(Sits on bed.)*

McQueen (*rummaging through pockets, emerges with money, which he throws at her*)   You can have a refund.

Shelly (*rising*)   I can *have* what I want. If I want you to crawl on your hands and knees and bark like a dog you will, because that's what you do, isn't it? Anything for money.

McQueen (*looks towards wardrobe*)   I don't want this any more.

Shelly (*goading him*)   But what about Sally? Does she want strange objects landing in her bag inside the supermarket? Does she want your kids picked up from school by a stranger? Ask yourself? I own you, you spoilt prick – (*Moving towards bed.*) – and you're not walking out on me. If I want you to follow me to Hawaii you will, because you're cheap. (*Lies on bed suggestively.*) Now come here and take off my panties.

McQueen   I'm not playing this game anymore.

Shelly   Yeah, yeah. (*She moves around seductively on bed.*) Come on, let's see what my money earns me.

McQueen   You disgust me. You call me cheap.

Shelly   Yeah, and you love it.

McQueen   You can threaten me all you want. You can play those games with my family, but it won't change anything. I'm not frightened any more and neither are they. Do you see? Are you fucking listening, Shelly, I'm not afraid of you any more. You don't do anything for me.

Shelly   I said come over here and do what you're good at.

McQueen   I'm out of here.

McQueen *moves away from window and walks towards the door.* **Shelly** *leaps off the bed and runs towards him, spins him round to face her, but he shies away.*

Shelly   What the hell's the matter with you?

McQueen (*facing away*)   I just don't want it any more.

Shelly   Come on, what's with all this drama? We do this every sodding time I come here. It's part of the game, isn't it? What's the matter with you tonight . . . I've never seen you like this. Is it the bloke, the one who belted you? Are you getting worried that my Richie'll find out?

McQueen (*facing her*) Maybe.

Shelly He'll never find out. He's married to a pint glass. He couldn't care less anyway.

McQueen It's too risky now . . . too sordid.

Shelly (*hugs him*) It's fun . . . it's different. It takes us away from the pissing rain and miserable bastards who haunt our streets. We could be in Vegas, LA, Sydney. We could be anywhere.

McQueen Hawaii?

Shelly (*excitedly*) Yeah, like we said. Hawaii . . . lying on the beach drinking cocktails and making love till the sun sets.

McQueen It's not real, Shelly. The truth is you're married, I'm married, and we have an arrangement. We live in the North East of England and our dreams die as soon as the sweat dries.

Shelly (*desperate*) It doesn't have to be like this.

She leads him back to bed. They sit down. She strokes his face and kisses his cheeks.

We can change it.

McQueen (*turning away*) Is that what you really want?

Shelly You know it is.

McQueen And you'd leave your husband and kids just like that?

Shelly Without a look over my shoulder.

McQueen (*facing her again*) What about your kids? You'd miss them . . . They're . . . they're part of you, for God's sake.

Shelly   We could have more.

McQueen   And your husband? You must love him. You couldn't just walk away from him, you'd break his heart.

Shelly   He hasn't got a heart.

McQueen   You must've loved him once.

Shelly   I never loved him. Never have . . . never will. I hate him. I hate him because he is everything you're not.

McQueen   I dunno, Shelly, I love my family. You know that. I like you . . . you're beautiful and smart and . . . but, I couldn't leave my family, especially like this.

Shelly (*desperate, clinging to him*)   Then divorce her. We won't see each other for a while, a few months, then we'll look as if we've just met and we'll hook up, like a couple, and we'll travel and . . . we don't need to worry about money. We'll kiss goodbye to −

McQueen (*freeing himself from her, walks around*)   I can't divorce her and I won't. I love my wife and I know you love your husband. The whole image is exciting. It's sexy and dramatic . . . like the movies, all this running off into the sunset, but that's all it is. It's just the next step from this fantasy you carry around inside your head.

Shelly   If I lose it I'll die.

McQueen   You don't need this, Shelly. You're a good woman with a lot to give. Don't waste it on something that's not there. (*Moves back to her, sits.*)

Shelly   I can't carry on,

Tears fall freely. **McQueen** *tenderly brushes them away. He then turns and takes a tentative, sneaky look towards the wardrobe and notices that it has opened very slightly.*

Shelly   I don't have the strength. I . . . I live for these meetings.

McQueen   Then we'll continue to meet.

Shelly   It's not enough.

Shelly *rises suddenly, paces stage, running her hands through her hair. She moves towards the handbag resting beside one of the beds. She wipes her mascared eyes and opens the bag. She emerges with a small gun, brings it out, her hand shaking. She waves it at him, mockingly.*

McQueen (*rising*)   Come on, Shelly, what's this?

Shelly   Our own little movie. You know how the cliché goes . . . If I can't have you . . .

McQueen   You've seen the movies, Shell, it doesn't work.

Shelly   Who cares?

McQueen   So no one wins.

Shelly   Something like that. Look, I gave you the chance. I've been giving you the chance for six months, and now you've made it pretty clear you just see me as a piece of meat.

Shelly *cocks gun and takes a few tentative steps towards* **McQueen**. *The gun shakes in her hand.* **McQueen** *moves forward and takes an anxious look towards the wardrobe, which is noticed by* **Shelly**. *She looks at him again, then back towards the wardrobe. After a few moments of deliberation she steps towards the wardrobe.* **McQueen** *takes a few anxious steps towards her, beginning to get edgy. Finally, when he thinks* **Shelly** *has sussed it all out, he screams out* **Hanson**'s *name.*

Suddenly, almost like slow motion, **Hanson** *emerges from the wardrobe.* **Shelly** *is so surprised, she takes a few steps backwards, the gun at her side.* **McQueen** *runs to corner of room.* **Hanson** *roars his anger and raises the bowie knife. He sinks it into his wife's chest as she manages to steady herself. She shoots one round into his stomach which knocks him back, and he falls into the wardrobe, the knife still in his hand. She then turns, mortally wounded, staggers, then fires a shot at* **McQueen** *who dives across bed, ducking just in time.* **Shelly** *staggers to a chair, and flops into it, dying.*

After a few moments, **McQueen** *gingerly emerges, shaking, checking his wound, surveys scene. He moves towards door, opens it, pops his head round and checks outside. All clear. He then moves towards*

Shelly *and drops down to check her pulse. To make sure, he takes a pillow from bed and smothers her, as all the time she tries to fight him off. He takes gun from her then looks towards wardrobe and sees* **Hanson** *struggling to rise.* **McQueen** *raises gun, moves towards* **Hanson** *who is still trying to get up.* **McQueen**, *calmly, kicks him to the floor and executes him.*

McQueen *walks centre stage, scratches his head in contemplation. He wipes off his fingerprints and puts the gun back into her hand. He then moves around the room like a whirlwind checking for any incriminating evidence. He moves things around, ruffles the bed, spreads some empty bottles around the room, knocks lamp over and scatters contents of table, trying to make everything seem like a domestic tiff gone wrong. He surveys the scene for a few more moments, breathing hard, trying to see that he has left nothing to chance.*

Finally, satisfied, he picks up his diary from floor and sits on bed, picks up phone, dials. His voice is different: gruff and guttural.

McQueen   Hey, baby, I'm gonna be a bit early tonight. I'm gonna be all yours . . . how's that? Get that champagne chilled and get yourself hot and steamy. Huh? My wife? My wife? Fuck that bitch, I don't give a shit what she wants. Who pays the fucking bills anyway? (*Laughs.*) Put those purple panties on and leave those titties hanging . . . you know that turns me on baby. See ya in about twenny minutes. You too baby, you too.

He replaces receiver, smiles, claps his hands in delight. He surveys the scene one last time, is satisfied that everything is sorted. He smiles smugly walks towards door, opens it, pokes head round, checks that he is okay then exits.

Lights fade on him and switch to **Hanson**, *dead. They rest on him for a brief moment, then fade slowly. Another light shines on* **Shelly** *for a moment. Just as the light is about to fade, her leg twitches violently.*

Lights snap off immediately.

End.

Printed in the USA
CPSIA information can be obtained
at www.ICGtesting.com
LVHW020931171024
794056LV00003B/712

9 780413 774798